Small Feet, High Mountain

The Story of Edith Wakumire

Margaret Spivey

AuthorHouse™ UK Ltd.
500 Avebury Boulevard
Central Milton Keynes, MK9 2BE
www.authorhouse.co.uk
Phone: 08001974150

© 2009 Margaret Spivey. All rights reserved.

No part of this book may be reproduced, stored in a retrieval system, or transmitted by any means without the written permission of the author.

First published by AuthorHouse 11/18/2009

ISBN: 978-1-4490-3581-5 (sc)

This book is printed on acid-free paper.

'How beautiful on the mountains are the feet of those who bring good news.' (Isaiah 52:7)

Contents

FOREWORD 1
INTRODUCTION. 3
1. 1950 ~ a motherless child. 5
2. 1935-50 ~ an untraditional family 9
3. 1950-3 ~ wicked stepmothers. 14
4. 1953-7 ~ life with auntie 18
5. 1957-61 ~ Edith goes to school. 25
6. 1962 ~ Independence Day – and murder. 31
7. 1962-6 ~ growing up 36
8. 1967/70 ~ Nabumali High School 40
9. 1971-3 ~ Idi Amin 47
10. 1973-7 ~ marriage, a baby, and university 55
11. 1977-80 ~ a country in turmoil, and a growing family. 63
12. 1980-5 ~ Solomon's eye, David's outreach 72
13. 1985-7 ~ AIDS and Singapore 77
14. 1987-9 ~ refugees, foundation of UWCM 85
15. 1982-2007 ~ Esaza's story. 92
16. 1990-91 ~ Edith's work expands. 96
17. 1991-2 ~ Edith goes to Europe, UWCM grows 100
18. 1993 ~ AIDS in the family; Edith goes to Canada 110
19. 1994 ~ the foundations of Faith House 115
20. 1995 ~ England, the churches and Solomon's eye. 121
21. 1996-7 ~ the President calls, but the pressures increase. 126
22. 1998 ~ the First Lady visits. Edith goes to New York 133
23. 1999 ~ the Silver Wedding. Community Mobilisation Teams established. 140

24. 2000 – a new venture, a further award, and Tamar's wedding. 145

25. 2001-2 – Edith to Brazil and Washington, Samson to Cuba 151

26. 2002-3 – Edith to Cape Town, then back to University 156

27. 2004-6 – the fight against malaria, Edith to Yorkshire and Wales. 161

28. 2006 – a Children's Conference, and more travels 166

29. 2007 – the trek, and my arrival. 172

30. 2007 – a day in the life of UWCM. 178

31. Jackson's story, Jacqueline's clinic 183

32. Canadian friends, the Porridge and Prayer Club. 186

33. Nancy and the school 192

34. The future. 198

BIBLIOGRAPHY 205

FOREWORD

I first met Edith Wakumire in 2006 when I took a team of people from North Somerset out to Uganda. I had heard of her work and was thrilled to be able to visit her and to see first-hand all that she is achieving in Mbale. We spent just two days with Edith but it was enough for me to appreciate the amazing character of the woman behind the work of UWCM.

Edith is one of those remarkable people, who readily inspires others to reach out and to do far more than they ever thought possible. It is surely no exaggeration to say that Mbale in particular would have been a very different place without her drive and enthusiasm.

She has done so much to fight the onslaught of HIV/AIDS and raise the status of women, helping them to achieve the rights they now enjoy in Uganda. None of it has been easy and she has suffered horrendous hardships and massive disappointments along the way. Two things have especially helped her – the love and support of her husband David and the inspiration and strength she has drawn from her deep faith in God.

Margaret Spivey has given us a huge insight into Edith's life and has helped us to understand how she has accomplished so much. The book has been meticulously researched and gives a detailed account of how Edith has been a significant driving force for change, empowering women and creating sustainable partnerships with others in order to fulfil her vision. Margaret interweaves it with stories that carefully describe Edith's family life and how she has challenged the values and customs of her own culture that have demeaned women. In so doing Margaret also gives us fascinating glimpses into Uganda's history and social make-up.

It is almost impossible to read this book without feeling thankful for the impact that Edith has had on so many people, and without being inspired and challenged by her example. Her many friends and supporters will be grateful to Margaret Spivey for opening up Edith's life to a wider audience.

Rev Tim Daniel
Director, Care for Uganda

INTRODUCTION

Edith Wakumire learned the hard way that women in Uganda were, both legally and traditionally, chattels to be bought and sold in a man's world. For most there was no option but marriage at first sign of womanhood, then child-rearing and endless work, usually in a multiple marriage. Widowed, they would be handed on to another male member of the family. Refusal could leave them homeless and destitute. The advent of AIDS brought added dangers.

Four influences have impelled Edith to help other women to change their destiny. Firstly, her father, called 'crazy' because he treated his wife and daughters with respect and sent his daughters to school. Secondly, her four sisters, who gave their unfailing love and support. Thirdly, her husband, David Wakumire, who broke with tradition to love and honour her as a valued, unique human being. Fourthly, her Father God and Saviour Jesus Christ, who is at the centre of their life together.

Today Edith speaks on the world stage as an authority on the relationship between poverty and HIV/AIDS. As well as her United Nations award, she received the World Vision International Robert W Pierce Award for Christian service to women and children in need.

Most of Edith's work is church-based, but she refuses to limit it by denomination or creed. She has challenged and changed church attitudes. Her ongoing creed is taken from the words in Micah 6:8:

> *'And what does the Lord require of you?*
> *To act justly and to love mercy and to walk humbly with your God.'*

I had the privilege of shadowing Edith in Uganda and met many of her family, co-workers and those they help, some of whom have since died. There will be gaps in my storytelling, but I have tried to paint a true picture of Edith's life as I and others see it.

Her story is an inspiration to all women to fight injustice, be strong and dream big dreams, not only for themselves but for others. Those small feet have grown, but they still climb mountains and bring good news.

NOTES

- I have used the word 'orphan' in the sense that most readers will recognise – someone who has lost both parents. However in Uganda a child who has lost one parent is known as an orphan, and the UN definition is a child under the age of eighteen who has lost either parent. Where I quote official figures the reader will understand that these people may still have one parent living.
- Most houses referred to are one, two or three-roomed mud-walled structures with a roof of either grass or banana leaf fibre.
- Multiple marriages, even among church members, are both legal and common.
- Human Immuno-deficiency Virus (HIV) multiplies quickly and can lead to Acquired Immuno Deficiency Syndrome (AIDS). Antiretroviral treatment (ARV) stops HIV multiplying, but it lays dormant and can be passed on. ARV must be taken for life, with food, otherwise its side effects (typically shaking) can be worse than the illness.
- Most figures I have given are taken from UNESCO reports.

For more information about Uganda Women Concern Ministry, please visit www.ugandaconcern.com

To make a donation towards Edith's work, cheques can be sent to UWCM UK Administrator, 1 Birch Avenue, Clevedon, North Somerset, BS21 7JT.

UWCM's NGO registration number in Uganda is 9514/552.

CHAPTER 1

1950 ~ a motherless child

The old woman hesitated on the threshold, blocking what little light there was inside the hut.

'Hello?'

'Is that Joyce? Come in.' Soferesi pulled a wooden folding chair out of a corner. A visitor was a rarity; she knew it wasn't her Joyce had come to see. The old lady stepped over the threshold, letting in a narrow strip of afternoon sun. Soferesi's reputation was more for hostility than hospitality. Childless, and long past the age when anyone would pay a dowry for her, she'd never fitted into the normal pattern of village life. She had a husband of sorts, but everyone knew she was there under sufferance.

Old Joyce sat on the folding chair. As Soferesi went to find her a mug of water, Joyce's eyes adjusted to the gloom and found the object of her visit. In the centre of the hut, a girl child sat on a folded grey blanket. Barely six months old, she had only recently acquired the art of sitting. Her round, sad brown eyes stared at this new face, searching hopelessly for the one face she would never see again.

'Poor little creature. What a terrible thing to happen. What's her name?'

'Edith. Edith Mary Muduwa.' (*Muduwa* means last born.)

'And it was all over in five days? What a shock for your brother.'

'Yes. Peninah was digging as usual, she cut her toe with the hoe and it went septic. By the time they got her to the hospital three days later it was too late. In two days she was gone. There was nothing they could do. And now he's left with this *malaaya* and four others.' (*Malaaya* means 'prostitute', a common way of referring to a girl child.)

Joyce nodded. How true. It just about summed up a girl's worth. What else are they good for? She took the mug of water from Soferesi, thanked her, and drank.

She knew all she needed to know of Soferesi's story. Soferesi kept the rest to herself. Philip was her half brother, same mother but different fathers. Both were scarred by a rough upbringing of neglect, jealousy and injustice. She'd had a series of 'husbands', thrown out first by one man and then another, never able to give one a child. Philip had taken her in whenever she'd needed help, and now it was her turn. They both knew their clan obligations. Gratitude didn't come into it.

'He's lucky he's got you to help him. But some of the girls must be old enough to marry or go to work, surely?'

Soferesi gave a harsh laugh. 'Work? Not them. He's the one who'll carry on working his fingers to the bone, just to keep them at school. He's crazy, working at the Coffee Co-operative just to pay for five daughters to go to school! It's a pity he ever got that scholarship to Nabumali High School, with its English teachers and big ideas. His *shamba*'s big enough to grow all their food, plus some coffee for a bit of cash. What's the point of working for somebody else as well? He should make his girls work. But he won't be told. '*Wekabuma*' ('having nothing')', that's what everyone calls him.'

'You're right; none of the girls in this village go to school.' She nodded at Edith. 'And it won't be long before this one can carry things, collect eggs, gather food, fetch water and dig. Then when her breasts start to show you marry her off for the best dowry you can get. Or send her over to Kenya. Plenty of *wazungu* (Europeans) there are looking for housegirls. Ten years is about the right age for that. The wages are good, and they can send a bit of money home.'

She didn't need to mention the other option. That was understood.

Edith was beginning to sway unsteadily. The old lady left her chair and picked her up, brushing the flies from the baby's damp face.

'She's not used to sitting up. She needs a bit of support. Or to lie down.'

Soferesi shrugged. 'Don't worry. I've seen plenty of babies even if I haven't had one of my own. I'll soon get the hang of it.'

'She's probably hungry.'

'I've got some porridge for her.'

Joyce sat down with the baby on her lap. Around the baby's neck Soferesi had tied a string, and on it were threaded a few coins with a hole in the centre, gifts of condolence from sympathetic visitors. Already Edith had been nicknamed *'Namugosi'*, the-one-with-a-string. Joyce fumbled in her pocket.

'Now, little *Namugosi*, let's see what I've got for you. Here's just a little gift to help the poor motherless mite.'

She untied the string, slipped a coin onto it and retied the knot. Then she handed the baby over to Soferesi and moved towards the door.

'Well, Soferesi, I wish you all the best. But you'd better tell that brother of yours he's letting himself in for a lot of trouble. And if you're the one who's going to bring up this little one, then you'll do it the proper way. The sooner she grows up and gets married, the better.'

Stepping out into the hot, bright African sunlight, Joyce shook her head sympathetically once again, then strode back to her own orderly life at the other side of the village.

Soferesi carried the now restless Edith back into the hut. She unfolded the blanket on the floor and lay the whimpering baby on it.

'All right, I know you're hungry. I'll get you something.'

She went through to the back of the hut where a little pot stood on the ground, covered with an enamel plate. She found a spoon and carried that and the pot back into the room, picked up the baby, sat down with her back against the mud wall, stretched her legs straight in front of her, and settled Edith on her lap. As the little girl snuggled closer, her head turned instinctively towards the dry, empty breast. With a brief impulse of pity and frustration her aunt let the child suck for a few seconds of closeness and warmth, but the comfort was short lived. Edith whimpered and turned her face away, still hungry and grieving.

Soferesi lifted up the pot and spooned soft porridge between the waiting lips. The child sucked and gulped, first eagerly, and then more slowly. Her eyelids began to droop. She gave a little hiccup and a burp. Soferesi put the pot and spoon to one side, shuffled across to draw the blanket further into the shade, and lay the baby down. She took the pot and spoon to the back of the hut, then turned and looked at her sleeping half-niece. She leaned over and fingered the string around the baby's neck, counting the coins.

'One more visitor and I'll have enough to buy a packet of cigarettes.' She smiled wryly to herself. 'It looks as if I've got my *malaaya* after all.'

CHAPTER 2

1935-50 ~ an untraditional family

Peninah shouldn't have died. After her funeral, when all the clan had finished stuffing their faces at Philip Koolo's expense and gone home, he tried to make sense of what had happened.

Death was common enough in a Ugandan village, but there was usually some obvious cause: dysentery, fever, cholera, or the slow, relentless decline of tuberculosis. But Peninah's accident had been a trivial one. And she was only thirty-six, young enough to have another child, perhaps a son next time.

Philip worked for the Bugisu Co-operative Union in the foothills of Mount Elgon, a vast, fertile region marking Uganda's border with Kenya to the east. It has been said that Mbale, its main town, was built on coffee*, and Bugisu was one of its biggest producers. Philip was one of a team of four who pruned the coffee trees and sprayed them with chemicals before sunrise every day. The pay may not have been high, but at least it brought some cash into the house. Peninah looked after the girls and cultivated their garden. It was a struggle, but with God's help they managed. And they were happy.

When the accident happened fifteen-year-old Florence was at school and ten-year-old Margaret was ill with a fever. She had always been a sickly child. Three-year-old Christine was playing with her baby sister. It wasn't the first time Peninah had cut a toe. She cleaned it as best she could and carried on digging. Three days later, her foot swollen and her temperature soaring, Philip took her to Budadiri hospital, three miles away. Leaving Margaret in the care of a neighbour, he took the other girls with him. When Peninah died of tetanus two days later, Florence took care of the two little ones while five-year-old Freda, the middle daughter, comforted her weeping father. Both were shocked. They had never seen a man cry before. They walked home over Butandiga Ridge carrying Peninah's body on their heads.

The villagers, always reluctant to admit that any death was from natural causes, were abuzz with rumours. Peninah must have been bewitched. Some even whispered that members of the Roman Catholic Church had bewitched her because they were jealous – she had been so prominent in the Church of Uganda, singing in the choir and a member of Mothers' Union (MU). Served her right for not worshipping with them.

Her funeral followed the traditional ritual. Members of the clan came from near and far and stayed for a whole week. The first day was spent finding food to feed them all. Florence and Freda dug up their crop of cassava, then cut bananas to eat and banana leaves for sleeping mats. By now Margaret seemed to be at death's door.

Peninah's body was on view for two days, then buried on family land. Three days of mourning followed. According to tradition no cooking was done, apart from the roasting of bananas. But the day before the clan's departure, chickens and goats were slaughtered at Philip's expense for a farewell feast. The banana leaf sleeping mats were ceremonially burnt, the house was swept, and the visitors departed.

Florence was a student at Nabumali High School, her father's old school a few miles south of Mbale, but now she stayed at home to take care of the younger girls. A slight deformity in one shoulder had made her right arm shorter than the other, but this didn't stop her digging. She always did more than her share of the work, however awkwardly. Florence's English was poor, but she was literate. And she had clever fingers. It pained her to see her sisters without food. One way she could help was by weaving baskets and mats from banana fibre and selling them, and the younger ones learned these skills from her to earn a few pennies.

Freda and Margaret, now recovered from her fever, carried on at school. Edith went to aunt Soferesi. It broke Philip's heart to let his baby go, but for the moment there was no alternative.

For Philip there was no question of replacing Peninah. Theirs had been more than the traditional arranged marriage. From childhood both had suffered the hurts, jealousies and frustrations of polygamous marriage; they were determined theirs would be different. Philip had looked at no other woman. Peninah had been content with him and their daughters. Together they had played an active part in church and community life. Philip had given a piece of land to build a church and school. As a Lay Reader one of his responsibilities was to prepare people for baptism. Both were natural teachers, Philip in the Men's Fellowship and Peninah in the MU, which had been in Uganda since 1914. To carry out this work, including counselling and preparing women for a church marriage, she would walk any distance. Both read lessons and sung in the church choir. On Sundays Peninah would change from her working clothes into traditional dress. The *gomas* is a long, square-necked gown with high pointed sleeve tops, and a wraparound front generous enough to be used as an emergency blanket or baby's shawl. With wide waist and head-bands in a complementary shade, the effect is dignified. At home they read the Bible, and the girls memorised Bible passages.

Philip taught the girls to sing, and they formed their own equivalent of the Von Trapp family, singing in harmony at church events. Philip had a beautiful voice, and Margaret would join him in singing the tenor parts. Freda remembers, 'They were the parents any child would love to have. They loved us so much, and made sure we grew up as Christians, loving one another, obedient, and respectful to elders.' When Philip heard people talk scornfully about the 'curse' of having five daughters, he would tell them that it was God who decided to give them girls. To Him there was no difference.

Few of the village children went to school, and Philip's girls went earlier than most. Florence would bring books home to show her sisters. On her first day at school Freda astonished the teachers by picking up a book and reading two whole sentences: 'See these children, Sarah and Moses. They are learning to read.' Florence had read it to her so many times that she remembered every word.

Christmas, Easter and baptisms were always times of feasting, not only for the family. Philip always insisted that they cook far more food than they could possibly eat. *Matoke* (green banana), rice, yams, cassava, chicken, beef, mushrooms, bamboo shoots, vegetables, and fruit, all were prepared for the big day. Their house was near the road, and passers-by, even to the Catholic Church a short distance away, would call to wish them happy Christmas or Easter, and be invited in for something to eat. Those in the village who couldn't afford meat knew where to go. The girls would have new clothes and loved showing off to the visitors.

Other men treated their wives as property, to be used or beaten for any tiny fault. Their puzzled wives would beg Peninah for some of the 'secret herbs' she obviously gave her husband to keep him calm.

Freda remembered just one terrifying moment when Philip came near to following the traditional pattern. They had been to a family celebration nearby and came home after dark. It had been a good feast, and they'd brought home a generous share of the leftover meat. As they approached the house Philip sent Florence ahead to light a lamp, but she ran back to say there was no oil. Philip had always insisted that Peninah give him at least one week's warning that something was running short. That gave him time to find the money to buy in economic quantities. While the neighbours would buy a small bottle of paraffin oil for a few pence, Philip bought a twenty litre tin. But Peninah had forgotten to tell him that it was running low. He was furious. For the first time ever, he raised his voice in anger.

'You deserve to be punished. Lie down at once. I'm going to cane you!'

Peninah hesitated for only a second. 'I'm sorry, and you're right; I was careless.'

And she lay down. The girls watched with horror. They knew this happened to other women. They'd heard the screams, they'd seen the swellings and bruises. But this was their father. The one who was different to all other men. The one who'd always taught them that they were valuable individuals.

For Philip this was a turning point, too. Seeing his wife on the ground, submissive, waiting for her beating, he was appalled to realise how close he'd been to breaking a lifelong commitment of love and trust. Choking back his anger and shame, he told his wife to get up. Nothing like that ever happened again. When Christine played with fire as a toddler and the house went up in flames, her father said that no-one was to blame. There was nothing to be done – except build another house.

Philip was a fastidious man. Every piece of cassava must be laid out properly, not overlapping or splashed with gravy. If one of the girls filled his plate sloppily he would hand it back to her. In the evenings, while the girls studied by lamp or candlelight (for the darkness falls suddenly at seven o'clock at this latitude), he would pull out an old biscuit tin from beneath a pile of neatly folded clothes. Inside the tin were a pen, a bottle of ink and an exercise book. With these he kept his accounts in the neat handwriting he'd been taught at Nabumali High School, recording his earnings from Bugisu and any profits from his own coffee crops. School fees, clothing, every penny he spent on kerosene, meat, soap or flour was recorded. Philip carried on this practice until he died.

Although Philip felt no urge to find another wife, he soon gave in to clan pressure to find a stepmother for his daughters. They were about to discover that wicked stepmothers aren't just characters in fairy stories.

*Andrew Purvis, *Observer Food Monthly*, June 2008

CHAPTER 3

1950-3 ~ wicked stepmothers

Male members of the clan found Anzerena Nabukwasi for Philip. All-male conferences were held (women play no part in such decision-making) and a modest dowry agreed. When Anzerena moved in only a few months after Peninah's death, Philip brought Edith back from her aunt's house.

In a photograph of the new family group, Philip appears dignified and composed, the only one sitting on a stool, his five daughters sitting on the ground in front of him. A short man of average build in his mid forties, he is neatly dressed in a light suit, with collar and tie. Fifteen-year-old Florence and three-year-old Christine form a protective shield around their plump baby sister, each holding one of her arms. Christine looks down at her. Florence is already a full-breasted, serious young woman, her eyes downcast and turned away from the camera. Margaret smiles, relaxed, while Freda, unsmiling, rests an arm on Margaret's shoulder. Behind the girls, next to Philip but on the ground and a foot away from him, sits Anzerena. She is a slight figure, probably not much older than her eldest stepdaughter, with small, sullen features. Even Edith's baby features show more personality than those of Anzerena. How does one gauge the emotions of a young woman married to a man at least twice her age, with five stepdaughters, one already a young woman? And those stepdaughters still in mourning for their loving, singing, warm-hearted mother?

Anzerena soon turned out to be the archetypal wicked stepmother, with her own cruel streak. She refused to cook or launder for the girls. Philip did his best to keep the peace. When he realised that Anzerena was eating every bit of meat he bought for the family, he would buy two separate pieces, a small one for her, a larger one for the girls. After cooking for herself while the girls were at school, Anzerena would let her fire die out, then deliberately dowse the smouldering embers. The girls would come home at four o'clock, having eaten nothing but a small bowl of porridge all day, to find no fire, no water, no food. Before they could cook they had to collect their own firewood and start a fresh fire. They took turns in cooking, and each would get up at two a.m. on her day to collect wood by moonlight, then find some way of keeping it dry. Every morning they would pray with their father, go out with him to dig, then at six o'clock bathe, dress and go to school.

The girls never told their father about Anzerena's cruelty. For a start, they doubted he would believe them. And if he challenged her with their accusations, she was mean enough to do something worse by way of revenge. He never knew that behind his back she referred to his daughters sarcastically as 'co-wives'. She became very cunning, disappearing whenever her husband was around.

Anzerena bore Philip a son, and they named him Christopher Nasufa. Soon after his birth she left for her parents' home, but Philip insisted that Christopher spend part of his childhood with him, and the girls were fond of their young half-brother.

Then Philip did something unheard of in Uganda. He took out that neat exercise book, turned over to a fresh page and wrote a will, leaving all his possessions, including land, to be shared equally amongst his five daughters (but not his son). He knew that to write a will was traditionally regarded as a death wish, but he also knew that when he died his daughters would be left with nothing. They'd be sent away penniless, at the mercy of any man who could make use of them. Male members of the family – uncles, cousins – would claim everything.

There was one more exception to this will. Freda, the healthiest of the girls, was very close to her father. When she worked alongside him before daylight in the coffee *shamba*, picking coffee beans together gave them a good opportunity for exchanging ideas. They discussed the importance of education, and the tradition of the dowry. Freda told her father that she didn't want to be traded for money or cows. Besides, only the men got anything of value: the women got their share of perishables only after the men had picked through them. Freda told her father about one girl who could only marry the man she loved if he gave her family a new Landrover as part of the dowry. Philip agreed that a girl should marry for love. Only after his death did she discover that although he had made limited provision for a dowry for his other daughters, she was excluded.

The older girls carried on at school. Edith stayed with Soferesi, sometimes alone, sometimes with Christine. During the school holidays they would all be together in their father's home, and those were the happiest times of all.

In 1954 Philip gave in to clan pressure once again and found another stepmother for his girls. As Christine later remarked, it was out of the frying pan, into the fire. Ezeresi Nabusiya was no more willing to take care of his family than Anzerena had been. Philip was very patient. Long before daylight he would get up and boil water for their coffee and porridge, then the girls would get up and work with him, either in their coffee *shamba* or amongst the crops of beans, bananas and cassava before he left for work.

Ezeresi soon started nagging Philip to send the girls away: she wanted them to start a new family of their own.

'Who will they go to?' Philip asked.

'Your relatives.'

'Soferesi is my only relative and she's already cared for the two youngest. I've no other sisters or brothers. It isn't the girls' fault their mother died.'

Ezeresi carried on sulking and wheedling, but Philip bided his time.

One weekend he invited her parents and her brother to lunch. Philip himself made an appetising meal for them. Everyone was very polite, but clearly they were suspicious. When the girls had cleared the dishes away, he waited until they were seated on the floor before he spoke. When he did speak, it was slowly, firmly, and without hesitation.

'Before you go, I want to ask you something. Can you please take these children with you?'

Startled, the girls looked at one another, then Ezeresi's father spoke.

'Why? We've given you our daughter to look after them.'

'I'll tell you why. Because your daughter refuses to look after them.

She's asked me to give them away so that she and I can have children. So now you must decide, when you leave this house, whether you take my daughters or your daughter.'

The girls listened, open mouthed. Surely he was joking? Ezeresi's parents were speechless, so Philip turned to her.

'You can go into the bedroom or anywhere in the house and pick up anything you want to take with you.'

Shaking, she stood up without a word, went into the bedroom, picked up her few belongings, then joined her parents and brother waiting in the doorway. All four walked away in silence.

Philip's girls were crying, and they hugged him. They'd always known he loved them. Now they understood that they were not only loved, but valued.

A few months later, Ezeresi gave birth to a son, a sickly child who died within a few days of birth. Even before the baby's funeral she went to visit friends in Kenya. Her mother stood with Philip at the tiny graveside, sobbing, cursing her absent daughter.

'She wouldn't take care of your children, and now her own has died. From now on she'll be cursed; she'll never have another child.'

And she didn't. Her second pregnancy was an ectopic one, and she never conceived again.

Florence left school and married Abednigo, a marriage that was to last happily for over fifty years. Very soon Edith was back with Soferesi, and this time Christine went with her.

CHAPTER 4

1953-7 ~ life with auntie

The next few years with auntie were unhappy, unsettled years. Soferesi, herself abused by an uncaring stepmother, was totally lacking in compassion. Later Edith and Christine joked that for every good word she spoke, there were nine harsh ones. One thing Soferesi taught the girls was how to greet an adult. A girl must go down on both knees before offering a hand to greet an adult. Both knees, not one: that would be a sign of disrespect. There was no such protocol for boys. If visitors arrive while parents are out, they must be invited to enter the house and sit down. Children must wait for the visitors to say what they've come for, and say nothing; it's disrespectful even to ask 'Can I help you?'

Edith kept herself in the background, never sure of who she was, never feeling like a complete person. People would refer to her in her presence as 'the orphan', 'the unfortunate one', still remembering her as *namugosi*, the one with a string around her neck. She caught all the usual childhood infections, including chicken pox, and, like all children, suffered from jiggers, a parasite that lays eggs under the finger and toenails, making them burn.

Apart from the little money Philip gave her, Soferesi was totally dependent on the 'husband' of the moment, moving in first with one, then another. Edith remembers four or five houses, four husbands. Each one treated her badly. She was a nagging wife, not afraid to beat her men with a stick. As Edith curled up on her mat each night, alone in the dark, with only a thin wall separating her from the adults, she heard the fights, the beatings, the arguments, and the men's harsh threats.

'This house and everything in it is mine. You brought nothing to it, and nothing in it belongs to you.'

Those words burned into Edith's memory. What really hurt was that she knew that everything the men said was true.

After a few months Soferesi would be thrown out, with no option but to trek back to Philip's village, taking Edith with her. Until she met another man who could use and tolerate her for a while.

The best times for Edith were the times Christine lived with them. Christine had a great sense of fun. They called Soferesi *Kuku*, which means 'Grandmother'. The first time they were evicted and marched back to their father's house, carrying their few possessions on their heads, Christine composed this marching song:

Nekuku asuda Isafari,
Eh! eh! Yayikola nga
Yomuzungu, eh! eh!

(Grandma, we're going on safari, Just like the *wazungu*, [Europeans], Marching like their porters, with their luggage on our heads.)

Edith and Christine would sing and dance and laugh, ignoring Soferesi's scowls and harsh shouts, 'Stop fooling, you two. Hurry up and shut up!'

It was always a relief to be with Margaret and Freda again. Although life was hard, they had a father who loved and respected them. They only had to look around the rest of the community to realise how rare this was. Florence would visit them as often as her housewifely duties allowed.

Philip had no time for male and female role-play. When it was Edith's turn to cook a chicken, she first had to catch and slaughter it. Each of his girls was taught 'man's work', even making *busera*, the local millet brew. In turn, he wasn't too proud to be a mother to them.

But with their aunt, they experienced the harsh life that was reality for every other girl in the village. Girls were told that certain foods were bad for them: if they ate lots of protein, such as liver and chicken, eggs or tripe, they would never menstruate. For men this tradition had two advantages: it saved money, and it prevented girls from growing too strong and independent. Children were given only the feet and heads of the chicken. To taste the meat they had to wait until the adults had finished – then suck the bones. When there was soup the children might get some of the broth, but only after the adults had scooped out the solids. (A UNICEF report of 2005 showed that in Uganda a third of women aged fifteen to forty-nine are anaemic, 10% of all women have a chronic energy deficit, more than half have Vitamin A deficiency.)

One day Soferesi roasted some peanuts and gave a few to Edith, just enough to whet her appetite. Soferesi hid the rest in a gourd, then went for a rest. But Edith knew where those peanuts were, and she was hungry. While her aunt was sleeping she tiptoed towards the gourd, mouth watering and tummy rumbling, lost her balance and knocked it over. Soferesi woke up. The first thing she saw was the fallen gourd, then the wide eyes of the terrified child. She screamed at Edith and gave her a hard smack. But casual cruelty wasn't enough for Soferesi. Warning the sobbing child to stay where she was, she rushed out into the garden, gathered a bundle of *Isula*, stinging weeds, then came back and beat Edith with them. Christine could only watch in horror as Edith's tiny body swelled, burning from the sadistic beating.

When Soferesi's man bought liver for the family, Soferesi warned the girls that it wasn't for children. If girls ate it they would develop a swollen spleen. Soferesi ate her share, smoked and dried what was left and hung it out of reach in the firewood store. The mouth-watering aroma drifted down to child level. Edith had the habit of sucking her fingers when she was distressed, and this was definitely a finger-sucking occasion. Christine didn't know which was worst – the smell of the liver or Edith's finger-sucking. The next day she could bear it no longer.

'Today I'll get some, and we'll both eat,' she whispered. 'You keep a look out while I get it. But whatever you do, don't tell *Kuku* or I'll beat you.'

Christine fetched two flimsy folding chairs, balanced one on top of the other, and climbed up both of them. From that height she could reach the top of the firewood stack – and the liver. But she was careful to leave some. What she'd taken she shared with Edith. It tasted so good. Whatever a swollen spleen was, it was worth the risk. When they heard Soferesi returning they ran out with innocent smiles to greet her, and Edith burst out: '*Kuku*, I've got to tell you, Christine climbed over the firewood store and picked the liver and we ate it and it was very nice.'

Christine got a beating from Soferesi, and Edith one from Christine. But Christine had the last word. Her body still stinging from the aunt's slaps she pleaded with her sarcastically, 'Next time don't hang the liver so high, or you'll make me fall.'

Which brought another slap. But it was worth it.

Without any explanation they were denied all their rights, whether to eat, talk or do anything that comes naturally to a child. They had learned one of the reasons children begin to steal – hunger. For the rest of her life Edith found food irresistible. Whatever was offered, she ate.

When Christine started school Edith, was left more and more alone with her aunt. As Soferesi grew older she became more desperate, and her men more callous. She started spending more time drinking *busera* with her friends. By now seven-year-old Edith was doing most of the hard work – fetching water, chopping wood, digging the garden and cooking food. One day Soferesi went out boozing with her friends, leaving Edith to make the supper. In Uganda, however meagre the fare, people are fussy about the flavour, using herbs and onions to make delicious gravy. Edith needed onion leaves, and went to look for them in the garden. Joe, the teenage son of Musa, Soferesi's current husband, looked up from his digging.

'What do you want?'

'I need some onion leaves.'

He put his spade down, wiped his hands on his trousers and stared at her thoughtfully. Although Edith was still small, her body was sturdy. Joe looked around: there was no-one else in sight. The boy's voice softened. He put a hand on her shoulder and turned her towards the house.

'You come back to the house with me, and I'll lie down with you, then I'll give you the onion leaves.'

Edith pulled away quickly. A child brought up in a small African house knows what happens when a man and a woman lie down together.

'No, I won't!' she shouted. 'And when *Kuku* comes back I'll tell her what you said.'

'If you do, I'll kill you!'

Edith stared him out. Joe was the first to turn away. He marched across to the onion patch, tore off a few leaves and thrust them into her hand. Nothing more was said, and Edith made the gravy.

After that she stayed as far away from Joe as possible.

Musa was at home a few days later when a neighbour rushed to the house, shouting, 'Come quickly, Musa. Soferesi's been drinking with another fellow and they've crashed his bicycle!' Furious, Musa ran to the site of the alleged accident, and met Soferesi on her way home. Perhaps she did have a drink with another man, but the accident was simple enough: the man had offered her a lift, the brakes had failed and the bike had crashed. The few grazes Soferesi had suffered were nothing to the cuts and bruises she got from Musa's beating. Soferesi crawled into the hut half dead and curled up on her mat.

Edith was terrified; not of Musa – she knew he was a cowardly bully. But if Soferesi died, what would happen to her? And Soferesi was obviously dying.

The child had a tender heart. Pity alone moved her to wash those cuts and put pads of cold water on the swollen eyes. She cradled the bruised head and trickled water through the bleeding lips. No one else came near the house. For two days she stayed in the house, nursing her aunt.

On the third day Soferesi was well enough to sit up. She began to show signs of returning to her normal irascible self, and ate a little food. In the evening Edith closed the shutters and lit a candle. Soferesi sighed loudly.

'My neck hurts. Get me some hot water, child. And I mean hot. And soap.'

Edith went out to the back of the house, built up a fire and stood a kettle of water on it, humming happily to herself. *Kuku* wasn't going to die after all. She remembered her father's teaching, and in her childish way said thank you to God for making *Kuku* better. Then in the dim glow of candle-light from the front room she rounded up all she needed. She poured the boiling water carefully into an enamel bowl, put the towel over her shoulder, tucked the soap under her arm and picked up the bowl. She heard the front door opening and voices murmuring in the other room. Visitors had avoided the house since the accident, but a neighbour must have popped in. Probably out of curiosity. Possibly to see what they could steal. There was only one thing: the candle. As Edith carried the bowl carefully towards the doorway, the light went out and the door slammed. The visitor and the candle were gone.

Edith stumbled. The bowl tilted. Boiling water splashed over her arms, hand, chest and stomach. She screamed, and then there was merciful blackness.

In its idyllic rural setting, white walls shaded and softened by the sumptuous blue blossoms of Jacaranda trees, Mbale hospital was a good place to spend the long healing process. But like most African hospitals it was poor. There was medical and nursing care, but no other services were provided. Families of patients had to feed, clean and clothe them. Florence had a husband to care for and could visit only occasionally, so Margaret was the one who walked to the hospital every day and took care of her sister. Each night for two months she slept on the concrete floor next to Edith's bed. It took a few days for Edith to come out of her coma and learn the full story.

When she heard Edith scream, Soferesi's first instinct had been self-preservation. She knew that whatever had happened to her niece, she would get the blame. Some fragment of folklore at the back of her mind warned her that she could go to prison for letting a child get burnt. So she kept Edith hidden for five days. She smeared Edith's body with yeast made from fermented millet flour, the only remedy she'd learned from village custom. First Edith's body swelled with enormous blisters, then bent double as the scalded skin contracted. The yeast and rotting flesh soon started to stink.

Now Edith tells her own story:

'A week after it happened, my aunt had to go out for a while, and Zerubaberi, my maternal uncle, happened to be passing by. He lived ten miles away, but was visiting another uncle and thought he'd call on us. He knocked at the door but there was no answer. Then he heard me cough. He called out, "Who's there?" and I answered, "It's me." He couldn't open the door. I crawled to the window and managed to open it. My uncle looked at me – and wept. Then he said, "I'm going to get your father." He cycled back home as fast as he could.

When Uncle Zerubaberi told them of my condition Dad came with two other uncles, bringing a folding canvas chair. They sat me on it. That is how they carried me to Buluganya dispensary. But there were no drugs there. They referred me to Mbale hospital, and somehow my father got me there. It took two months for my body to heal.

'When I came home from hospital my Dad was so happy that he slaughtered a chicken and prepared nice soup for me. Because of what my aunt had made me believe about women eating chicken, I told my father, "I don't eat chicken", but I saw my sisters eat and enjoy it. I found that puzzling. There was some left over, so when they were all away I stole some and ate it. It was good! They returned to find some pieces missing. "Did you have some of this chicken?" they asked, but I denied it. Later Dad talked to me and asked me what had really happened. I confessed that I'd tried some to see how it tasted. He was amused. He understood me so well. In fact he bought another chicken and cooked it especially for me. I still thank God for an understanding father who would listen, explain and guide. Yes, children really need a father. His action freed me. It helped me not to hide or be hypocritical, either about chicken or women.'

Despite Margaret's care there were fears for Edith's future. Her chest had been badly scalded. If the breast 'buds' had been destroyed, what man would want a woman with no breasts?

But Edith had already decided she would never marry. She'd seen women in the community, battered, abused, living in fear, with no property or security.

She took it for granted that she'd have to go back to her aunt, but when she mentioned this Margaret exploded,

'You want to go back to the one who left you nearly dead? And how are you going to suckle children when your whole chest is burnt?'

No, there was no question of her going back to Soferesi. Or marriage. Life was going to be difficult. Their father had to work, the other girls were at school, but somehow they would manage. They always had.

CHAPTER 5

1957-61 ~ Edith goes to school

Edith's scars healed surprisingly well. Once she'd recovered from her injuries she had to help with the work again, but this time she was rewarded with her father's thanks and a smile. And she was entitled to her share in the proceeds.

The one job Edith hated was pounding peanuts. Dried fish with peanut sauce – cheap, tasty and nourishing – was one of her father's favourite dishes. Whenever Edith saw him bringing dried fish home, she knew she'd have to pound peanuts for the sauce. So she would hide in the latrine, a handy place to pass the time. And far pleasanter than anyone could imagine. One of the many useful things her father had learned at Nabumali High School, as well as good English and neat handwriting, was how to keep a latrine clean and sweet-smelling. Whenever visitors had used it, Philip would send one of the girls to make sure they'd left it as he would wish to find it. Every day a dry banana leaf would be set alight, the smoke wafted around to kill any offensive odours. Philip even spent some of his precious income on Jeyes disinfectant. There was a metal cover over the seat of the latrine, and there Edith would sit, thinking about life, singing a little song to herself.

Another enjoyable way of wasting time in the latrine was the game of 'Stones'. That's where you pick up a small stone, throw it in the air, and catch it on the back of your hand. Then you pick up two stones, and try to catch them both. If you're very adroit you can catch five at a time, but Edith's hands never grew big enough for five. It was amazing how pleasantly the time passed playing Stones. But once Margaret discovered her secret, she would go straight to the latrine and hammer on the door.

'Come out of there at once, you bad girl. I've got a job for you; I know you're there.' Margaret would give her a slap and a good telling off, then throw the stones away. But there were always more stones where those had come from.

Philip still sang in the church choir. Their home was a lively, welcoming place, and Edith learned from her father how to get on well with people. She enjoyed playing with boys. But people were suspicious of a man who treated five daughters as human beings. And possibly jealous of the way they worked so well together. It was a tradition in their village that for Christmas all the families would share the cost of buying a cow. When it was slaughtered each family would take their share of the beef, a rare treat. One Christmas Philip had spent all his money on school fees; there wasn't enough left to pay for his share of the cow. However he had enough to pay for a small portion. He sent one of the girls with his last few coins, but she came home still holding the coins – and no meat. The villagers had told her; 'Tell your father if he didn't waste money on school fees for girls he could afford to buy a whole cow. He must either pay for his full share or go without.' That Christmas they had a chicken for dinner, but they thanked the Lord all the same.

By now Freda was at Bubulo Girls' High School. Edith wasn't strong enough to walk the long distance to primary school. And there was the cost. A child needed a uniform, exercise books, pens and other equipment on top of the school fees. So for the next few months Edith went to the little church school built on the land her father had given. Here there were no desks, uniforms or exercise books. On sunny days the children sat outside on the ground and write in the dust with their fingers, or in the rainy season they would shelter under the grass roof and scratch on a banana leaf. It was a surprisingly effective system. Little fingers would write '2 + 1 = 3' in the dust, and teacher would make a tick with her finger. Or in the case of '2 + 1 = 4', a cross.

Primitive as it was, the system worked and Edith soon picked up the rudiments of literacy and numeracy. Their father taught all of them to know God. Whenever his work allowed, they would start each day with prayers, and again before the evening meal. Each of the girls took turns to lead prayers, read the Bible and introduce a song. By the time Edith was nine she was strong enough to make the long walk to school, and her formal education began. But she'd already received a good grounding.

It was a proud little girl who put on her school uniform in 1959 and set off with the other children, proud especially that Freda had worked so hard to help her to get there. Besides the bursary she had won for her place at Nabumali High School, Freda earned pocket money by gardening and car-washing for one of the teachers. Every morning the children ran the seven miles to school over the mountain, bare footed, singing and joking all the way. It seemed like no distance at all, and took them only an hour. Best of all, Christine was one of the merry party on this daily journey. Although the track was through wild bush country, animals such as baboons and snakes kept their distance and the children never felt threatened.

Edith's school reports show that she was given the name Mary Edith Muduwa. 'Muduwa' means the last born, and this name has stayed with her. It was more than a nickname. Every child is given a name that signifies its place in the family. But they all had nicknames as well. Edith was still called by her baby name, '*Namugosi*', the one with a string around the neck. Aunt Soferesi nicknamed Margaret '*Wolayo*', the one who reached death and came back, and Freda '*Wegosasa*', the different one – because she didn't look much like any of her sisters. Christine was known as '*Wogyoka*', the one who set the house on fire.

Those seven years at Bulaago were happy, but hard. Much of the family income depended on that precious cash crop grown in their family *shamba* – Arabica coffee. The coffee bush is a graceful plant, with long, slender stems and dainty, glossy leaves, but there was never time to stop and admire it. Edith's working day started an hour before the sun had fully risen. She joined the adult village co-operative, digging first in one farm and then another. (75% of the population of Uganda depend on agriculture for their livelihood, and women contribute more than 70% of the agricultural labour force.) When it was the team's turn to work in Edith's *shamba*, she would cook for them. The red coffee beans were picked, pulped, then left in water to ferment. After two days the pulp was removed from the husk, and the beans washed. The team would pick out the good beans, carry them home, then lay them out to dry on a wide elevated tray, six foot long, and light enough to carry indoors in case of rain. To speed up the drying process Philip made long-handled scrapers for his girls to reach across the tray and move the beans. Finally the dried beans were taken to the co-operative market, where they were carefully graded. Edith and her sisters took great pride in their father's teaching, and always got the top price for their Grade 1 coffee.

After work, Edith would eat the breakfast her father had prepared, drink the coffee he had left simmering, then wash and change into her school uniform. The big problem was perpetual hunger. The half bowl of thin, undercooked porridge the school provided did little to relieve their hunger pangs, and the seven-mile homeward run on an empty stomach was almost unbearable. So Christine and Edith would save a little from the evening meal, perhaps potato and bean mash, wrap it in banana leaves, tuck the parcels into their school bags and hide them in the bush near the school. After they'd eaten their meagre midday porridge, they would sneak out and dig up their treasure hoard. Their secret feast became a high spot of the day. One day some animal, probably a rat, had got there first and eaten half. But they enjoyed whatever was left.

There was another way of raising cash at the weekends: bamboo shoots. But these had to be cut where they grew, deep in the mountain forest. This meant skipping school on Fridays. Sometimes Edith would spend Thursday night at a friend's house near the school, then get up at 5 a.m., sneak past the school carrying a knife and some *matoke* (steamed green banana) wrapped in a banana leaf. Crossing first one mountain ridge then another, she would reach the bamboo forest and start cutting the delicate shoots, stacking them in a bag over her back. By noon the *matoke* was rotten, but she ate it anyway. After dark she carried that precious load back over the mountain. She was often scared out of her wits, hearing wild animals crashing through the undergrowth or the shouts of bandits in the distance. One night, the longest and worst night of all, she got lost. Hungry and scared and with bleeding feet, somehow she found her way out; if either she or Florence didn't get the precious load to Buluganya market by Saturday morning, the whole weekend would have been wasted.

As the years took their toll on Soferesi's attractions her visits to

Philip's home became more frequent. The older girls now began to feel the sting of her tongue. She was totally unpredictable. If they brought friends home she would demand, 'What are you doing here?' If she asked one of them a question, and they gave a reasonable answer, she would snap at them, 'Don't answer back.' If Edith came home from school hungry and cut herself a banana, Soferesi would shout at her, 'How dare you?' If she didn't, then said she was hungry, Soferesi would snarl, 'Then why don't you get yourself a banana, stupid?' Edith soon learned never to refuse any food that was offered, or there for the taking.

As if five daughters weren't enough, Philip also took the daughter of a distant relative under his wing. Enida was the same age as Margaret. Philip treated her exactly as he had treated his own girls. Members of the clan thought he was crazy when he paid for her education right up to the point of teacher training college. And when she became pregnant in her final year and couldn't finish the course, he was an even bigger laughing stock.

'The idiot! There'll be no bride price for her now: he's wasted all that money on a prostitute.'

'You're right, and his own girls are bound to go the same way!'

Philip's generous heart was forgiving, but he had to spend most of his working hours away from home, so it was Soferesi Enida had to contend with. Soferesi would beat her, then make her eat at the back of the house with her baby, not with the family. This, too, was tradition. The other girls took it for granted that *Kuku* knew best. But they didn't like it.

Edith covered two years of schooling in her first year at Bulaago, and stayed there for seven-and-a-half years. Then she went on to Buhugu Primary School for two terms before sitting her Junior Leaving Certificate of Education. Freda paid these fees for her and Christopher. These were years of hard work both in school and in the field, but at least the family was together, and their singing, worship and joy in one another carried on undiminished.

There were signs that those fragile breast buds hadn't been irreparably damaged after all, and Edith's attitude to marriage began to change. She started to pray about this. She asked God to find her a very special man with the same character as her father, a Christian who valued women and girls. She prayed, 'God, if I am to marry, let him be a poor man, and then we can work together to develop something. So that if a man beat me or said anything bad, I could tell him, "my friend, we have worked together for these things, so there is no way you are going to abuse me." And God, if you gave me a man who ever beat me, even one slap, that would be the end of marriage in my life.' And she kept reminding God of this.

Yes, perhaps she would get married after all. But first she had to get herself an education.

CHAPTER 6

1962 ~ Independence Day – and murder

On 9 October 1962 wide banners and tall shields in black, yellow and red, the colours of the new Uganda flag – black for the colour of the people's skin, yellow for sunshine, and red, the blood of brotherhood – framed every road leading into Kampala. The country's new flag with its emblem of the Crested Crane, Uganda's tall, proud and dignified native bird, flew triumphantly in every town. If people in remote villages hadn't been able to obtain the new flag, any flag would do. This was a time for celebrating, not for splitting diplomatic hairs. But in Kampala the Union Jack was lowered for the last time. Uganda was now an independent republic ruled by the Uganda People's Congress, with Milton Obote as her first Prime Minister, and the Kabaka Edward Mutesa II her first President.

Even in villages far away in the foothills of Mount Elgon, there was rejoicing, but for most people daily life went on as usual. Edith was now twelve years old, making good progress at school and working as hard as ever in the *shamba*. She was now the oldest child at home, and when it was time to harvest the coffee she would employ a team of workers to help her, paying them off when the beans were sold.

Margaret, still single, now worked as a salesgirl at Zeema Trading Centre in Mbale, and lodged with a cousin nearby. Freda was at Nabumali High School, preparing for her Cambridge School Certificate exams in November. Christine was in Junior 2 at Bubulo Girls' School. The neighbours still called Philip '*Wekabuma*', especially now that he'd taken in Nadunga, a girl cousin of Edith's age, as well as his young son, Chris. But all five sisters had good reason to be optimistic about the future.

Philip had been promoted to foreman at Bugisu. He would get up while the children were still asleep, build a fire in the outdoor kitchen and make porridge and coffee for them. All this he did on 12 November.

That morning Edith was first of the children out of bed. She went to the latrine, then towards the place where the hot coffee and porridge were usually waiting.

The sun was still low, and Edith almost tripped over her father's body. But there was enough light not to mistake the blood trickling from his head, or the slowly congealing blood darkening the ground around him. Perhaps he'd had a nose bleed and fainted. Edith touched his shoulder, giving him a shake. Only when she turned him over and tried to pull him up did she see the machete cuts. She screamed, then ran through the village shrieking, 'Help, somebody's murdered my father!' Stumbling, sobbing and still screaming, she ran to Margaret's house. Margaret tried to calm her. How could father have been murdered? He hadn't been robbed, had he? She ran back with the hysterical girl to see for herself. It seemed incredible. But it was true. Although their father's killer (or killers) had also ransacked the house without waking the children, nothing had been taken. Margaret sent for the police, but they didn't arrive until the evening.

That day Christine was dinner prefect at her boarding school when someone handed her a letter written by her father the week before. She slipped the envelope in her pocket, waiting until all the diners had left before opening it. Then she skimmed eagerly through the usual family stories. But it ended with some upsetting news: one of their close neighbours had been murdered. Christine was horrified; how could something so dreadful happen so close to home? Fighting back the tears, she put the letter back in the envelope. As she was about to leave the dining room she glanced out of the window to see a familiar car pulling into the school compound. Her cousin Abednigo was at the wheel. He'd never visited the school before. He could only have come for some bad reason. Christine waited in the dining room, shaking with fear.

Abednigo went first to the teachers. They found Christine in the dining room, now sobbing, not knowing why, still clutching her father's letter. Abednigo broke the devastating news to her, then drove her to Nabumali High School to collect Freda.

The village was still in an uproar. The police made a cursory search of the area, then took Philip's body to the mortuary in Mbale. Edith, Nadunga and Christopher drove with them to Mbale police station and sat there for hours, frozen with grief and horror.

It was two days before the body was released for burial, and when they got home they began to suspect a motive for the murder. There was no doubt it was premeditated. Whoever had attacked Philip had climbed a big tree outside the house before daylight, waited until he left the latrine, and dropped on him with a machete. But now the house had been ransacked again, not by robbers, but by the extended family. According to custom, the men were rightful inheritors of whatever property Philip had left.* The few pieces of furniture and cooking pots had disappeared. The doors had been left open, and thieves had moved in and started to pull the house apart. Each of the relatives had assigned himself part of the *shamba* and coffee plantation. Some were hacking ripe bananas off the trees to carry away, calling out to one another as they worked, 'Stupid man, with all this, wasting money to educate five *malaaya.*'

Philip's daughters could only sit on the bare floor and wait to hear what was to become of them. The four unmarried girls were now the property of the male members of their father's clan.

But Soferesi had given cousin Abednigo Philip's notebook. After the funeral Abednigo gathered the family around him and showed them the book. When he told them it contained Philip's will, written in 1956, they were aghast; Philip had signed his own death warrant. Then Abednigo dropped his bombshell. The will bequeathed an equal share in everything he owned, including coffee plantations and land, to each of his five daughters. The will was unsigned and undated, but it was written in the same book as his financial records, all in date order and in the same neat hand. There was no denying its legitimacy. They listened in silence as Abednigo read its contents slowly and clearly. Philip had violated their culture, and there was nothing they could do about it. But they would keep quiet for the time being. There were still the dowries to look forward to: they saw no reason why they shouldn't have a share of those. They hadn't noticed that Freda's name had been excluded from the dowry arrangements. Soferesi was satisfied that Edith's dowry was to include a cow for her. By the time Abednigo had finished the relatives had all tiptoed away.

The suspicion began to grow that Philip's murder had been a hired killing. The police picked up a suspect from a neighbouring village, but there were no witnesses, and the case was dropped. Their chairs and cooking pots were never seen again.

It may seem strange that Philip's only son was left no share in his father's property. This was probably a wise decision. To bring the child of a disgruntled ex common-law wife into the equation would probably have led to long and bitter feuding. Chris stayed with Edith in Soferesi's care for the next three years, and the sisters helped whenever they could, but after their father's murder he played a diminishing role in their lives.

The sisters got on with life as best they could. Freda was persuaded to go ahead with her O level exams two weeks after the funeral. Sobbing all the way through the exams, and spoiling many of the papers with her tears, she managed to scrape a Grade II Cambridge School Certificate, then moved to Gayaza High School in Kampala, staying with the cousin of an old school friend. Florence was with her husband in another village. Margaret kept an eye on things.

Now head of the house, twelve-year-old Edith still had to carry on with her work and school, but her loss was almost unbearable. The teaching in their church had been rudimentary. It would be another five years before Edith heard the word 'salvation'. She remembers: 'Among the things my father taught us, he said that when a Christian dies, he will have life again. I took this literally. When Dad died I did not take it seriously because I knew that one day he would come back. They always come back.' So Edith would hurry along her father's homeward path every evening and wait for him. For a month she waited in agony of hope and despair.

When Margaret came to visit one evening Edith asked her, 'Sister, what happened to Daddy? Why doesn't he come back?'

Margaret realised that nothing but a cold splash of truth would free Edith to move forward. She led Edith out of the house and took her to her father's grave, alongside that of her mother a few yards from the house.

'Look, Edith, this is where we buried Daddy's body. He was killed. He died, just like Mummy. She'll never come back and neither will he. I know the Bible says they will, but that's not true. They don't really come back.'

Edith had thought the day of her father's murder was the worst day of her life, but this was even worse. She'd lost not only the person she loved most, but her whole future. There was nowhere else to turn. All she could do now was to go as a nanny or housegirl in Kenya. She wept for two days. Then Margaret comforted her.

'Edith, it's true Daddy has died, but we're still alive and God will take care of us. And just think about your sisters getting a good education. Do you think God won't help them to finish school, and then help you? So don't despair. God will help you.'

Edith tried to believe this last promise, but it was difficult. Her father's earnings at Bugisu couldn't be replaced. All she could do now was work even harder in the coffee *shamba*, cultivate the rest for edible crops, and somehow struggle on at school.

The coffee paid her school fees for the next few years. At the right season, Edith would carry two heavy tins of coffee on her back from their village, over one mountain ridge, across the valley and up the next ridge to the main road, a two hours' walk, for which she got paid 50 cents. Freda, Christine and young Christopher would also carry a load. But without Florence's help this casual labour would not have been enough to live on. When the crop was ripe Florence would walk the long mountain walk to collect the beans, carry the heavy load back across the mountains, dry them and deliver them to the coffee co-operative.

Edith thanked God for Florence's sympathetic husband; few other men would have allowed their wives to leave home for days as he did. And he helped financially as best he could. She also thanked God that her father had had the forethought to make a will. Perhaps she could trust Him with the rest. She began to face the future with some kind of hope, and worked even harder in the *shamba* and at school for the next five years.

*Daughters had no legal right to inherit until 5 April 2007.

CHAPTER 7

1962-6 ~ growing up

After Independence the country still faced years of turmoil. But life went on much as ever in rural Uganda. Political strife and treachery in far-away Kampala made no difference to Edith.

Life was hard. Sometimes Soferesi would go out drinking, then bring home a man. She would wake Edith up, ask the man to give the money to Edith, then have sex with him. It was a gross humiliation for Edith to be used as her drunken aunt's banker.

Soferesi could never offer love, but at least she gave some protection, especially to Edith and Nadunga, who stayed with them for a while. By now Margaret was married to John Ssonko. She and Florence did what they could to help, but both had their own families to care for. The children had to work even harder to cultivate food to fill their bellies and the precious coffee crop to pay school fees.

Edith's chances of a good education had depended upon Freda's progress. When Freda became pregnant in 1964 and left school, all Edith's hopes were shattered. Who was there left for her to trust? Edith ran into the plantation, sobbing, 'I'll end up like all the rest. Men will make use of me, call me a prostitute.' Then a feeling of peace enveloped her. She realised that her future was in her own hands – and God's. Although she was only a nominal Christian she prayed, 'God, help me not to do that. Please help me to become a success in life.' She wouldn't let boys near her. Neighbours called her *Mulokole*, which means literally 'saved', but can also mean 'spoilt'. She was putting herself above the rest, refusing to accept her traditional role as a woman.

Freda's overwhelming shame was that she had let her father down; he'd had such high hopes of her going to university. She botched two abortion attempts. She couldn't even commit suicide successfully. For several days she sat on the railway tracks hoping to be sliced to death, but somehow her timing was never right. Later she came to believe that she and her baby girl were under divine protection. One reason was the support of her headmistress, Joan Cox. When Mrs Cox found out why Freda had left school, she made the four-hour journey from Kampala to Mbale to see her. She urged Freda to leave George, the baby's father, giving her money and an expensive new suitcase. Freda had already reported George to the police for slapping her, but they had told her this was a domestic issue. George spent all of Mrs Cox's money, and after a final argument burnt all Freda's belongings, including clothes, education certificates – and the new suitcase. She left carrying nothing but the baby, who she named Joanne after Mrs Cox.

On 14 December 1964 Edith, now a small, skinny fourteen-year-old, was presented with her Primary School Leaving Certificate. She went on to Bulaago Junior Secondary School, where she passed her Junior Leaving Exams, then to Buhugu for her final six months for her O levels. That year a young, newly-qualified teacher named Phenehas had started work at a nearby school, and Freda arranged for Edith to stay in his house, doing housework for him in lieu of rent. There were three teachers and six children in the house, so Edith felt both valued and safe. Phenehas found Edith very mature and easy to talk to. She was inquisitive, and often took her problems to him. Their friendship was to last a lifetime. Later Phenehas married Florence, Edith's Home Economics teacher, who taught Edith embroidery. By the time she married she had a huge pile of embroidered tablecloths in different colours for each day of the week.

Edith's new self-confidence stood her in good stead on three occasions in the next few years.

For a girl between the ages of twelve and fifteen, danger is never far away. In 1964 she was staying with Christine and her husband during the school holidays. One day they were all going to a party, but Christine was working late, so she sent her husband to collect Edith on his motor bike. Alone in the house with Edith, prettily dressed and ready to go, he locked the door. She realised immediately what kind of party he had in mind and fought her way out of the house, screaming, 'I'll tell my sister!'

'If you do, I'll deal with you,' he snarled, but he let her go. He knew there were strong muscles under that soft brown skin.

From time to time Edith had to go home from Buhugu to collect food from the *shamba*. A neighbour saw her leaving one evening with an overnight bag, and asked her in friendly fashion where she was going. He strolled alongside, chatting, then told her he knew a short cut. Edith knew he was married. She trusted him. After a while he stopped outside a house.

'Some of my friends live here; let's just go in and say hello,' he said.

Edith didn't notice the signals that passed between them. After a few minutes the family made excuses and left the two alone. Edith put up a mighty struggle and escaped, leaving her bag behind.

Margaret's husband was the first of a number of men who were to be father figures to Edith. John knew what his small, skinny sister-in-law had endured, and became a source of strength to her. To him she would pour out all her hopes and needs, and he always treasured the letters and reports she sent him from school.

While John was teaching in a private school in Tororo, Edith went to visit him and Margaret. One rainy day another teacher found Edith alone, pulled her into his room, and tried to force her, but once again she escaped after a fierce struggle. Edith might have been forgiven for despairing, but she'd suffered too much for too long, and wasn't about to give in now. She remained a virgin until her marriage.

These teenage experiences built up Edith's determination in later years to create a society in which vulnerable young women were protected – and respected. As things were they were totally at the mercy of men, with no rights or property, bought and sold like cattle – but without the value of cattle. She had already seen how degrading and dangerous many traditions were for women, especially those of widowhood.

A widow must put on her deceased husband's shirt inside out, then tear a strip off it to tie around her head at the funeral. She's not allowed to grieve or eat cooked food with her children, but must eat roasted bananas on her own for one week, then go through a 'purification' ritual. For this she must dress up seductively, putting on any perfume, jewellery or makeup she may have, then go into town, find a man – any man – and have sex with him. Thus 'purified' she can return home and resume contact with her children. (It's believed that if you eat with your children without 'purification', they will die.) She is then 'inherited' by a male member of her late husband's clan, even the son of an older wife.

On the birth of twins a wife is obliged to 'celebrate' by having sex with another man in the clan. In a multiple marriage, a neglected wife may look elsewhere for sexual favours or financial supporters. A barren woman is regarded as cursed. She will do anything to become pregnant, including having sex with the witch doctor by way of payment. If she's unfortunate enough to bear a succession of daughters, she may do the same in an attempt to have a male child. Much later Edith was to recognise the part these traditions played in the spread of HIV/AIDS. She taught that a woman can choose to say 'No' to sex, even with her husband, when he's been with another woman, exposing his wife to the possibility of AIDS. It isn't easy, but her life may depend upon it.

If a girl becomes pregnant before marriage she's called 'cursed', even by the father of her baby. Often her only way to survive is to turn to prostitution.

Two months after giving birth Freda left her baby daughter with a friend and did a secretarial course at the Uganda College of Commerce. In April 1965 she got a job as Stenographer/Secretary, enabling her to help Edith with clothes and pocket money. In 1966 she won a scholarship to the Gregg Secretarial College in Ealing, London, then on to a two-year teacher training course at Huddersfield Technical College (now a university) in Yorkshire. She came back to Uganda with a Certificate in Office Arts from Leeds University, qualified to teach at Nakawa Secretarial College, Kampala.

In 1966 Prime Minister Milton Obote clashed with the President, Kabaka Mutesa II. Fearing the Kabaka's influence, Obote called on Idi Amin, his army Chief of Staff, for help. Amin was from the West Nile district near the Sudan border. He stormed the Kabaka's palace: the Kabaka fled to London. Obote arrested several of his ministers, proclaimed himself President and abolished the monarchy. The Constitution was suspended, and in 1967 Uganda became a republic.

And when Christine started work as a secretary in 1967, Edith's bamboo-cutting and coffee-rearing days were over.

CHAPTER 8

1967/70 ~ Nabumali High School

Edith couldn't believe it: she was actually a student at her father's old school, Nabumali High. She stepped across the threshold early in 1967, bursting with pride. Nabumali was a missionary school with a long reputation for good teaching and discipline, and an English headmaster, Mr Ron Wareham. Although Edith had heard much about the school, the difference between life there and the life she'd known so far, with its desperate daily struggle to stay alive, was beyond the young girl's wildest dreams.

For a start, she no longer looked like an orphan. She had three uniforms – one for class, one for cleaning and gardening, and a white one for Sunday. And for the first time in her life she wore shoes – shiny black ones. No more jiggers and bleeding toes!

Saturday is market day in Nabumali Corner, a busy stopping place on the road south between Mbale and Tororo. People come from miles around to buy and sell. The road is choked with stalls, food produce, sandals, blankets and clothing spread out on every inch of ground, even hanging from ropes suspended across the path. There's little chance of any vehicle wider than a bicycle battling its way through. Nabumali High School is about half a mile away up this narrow, twisting, potholed road. The school itself had a village atmosphere, with classrooms, staff houses, separate dormitories for five hundred boys and girls as well as a wide variety of sports fields. Prominent amongst the buildings was St Peter's chapel. Church attendance on Sundays had once been compulsory, but this rule had been dropped the year before Edith joined.

The school boasted a new swimming pool, officially opened in 1965 by the Minister for Education. Older students still laughed when they told Edith about that day.

'We thought the Minister would just turn up looking all solemn, wearing a suit and tie. He'd make a long, boring speech, cut the ribbon, then we'd all cheer and that would be it. Well, we were wrong. For a start he stepped out of the car wearing a dressing gown, and when he'd made his speech and cut the tape, he stripped off to reveal a pair of swimming trunks. Then to everyone's horror he climbed up to the 15ft board, took a dive and belly flopped into the pool. There was water everywhere. The boys all yelled and the girls screamed. We waited for the blood to spread through the water, but he came up with a big grin.' The school had every kind of sports team, including cricket, netball, hockey and football.

At Nabumali there was fun. The school had an outdoor stage, where dramas such as *Volpone, As You Like It* and *The Merchant of Venice* were staged. The language of Shakespeare presented few difficulties for students taught from the King James Bible and the 1662 Book of Common Prayer. The wife of one English member of staff gave birth while she was there, and was delighted when a local member of staff approached her with the greeting, 'Madam, I believe you have brought forth.' Edith took part in the dramas, not caring whether she had a small part or simply helped backstage. All that mattered was to be part of the team. The young people enjoyed an occasional treat when a film was projected onto the side of the building above the stage. Edith was thrilled with *The Student Prince*, especially the singing. A favourite for all was any of the Tarzan films. Alongside the outdoor stage a fishpond was the favourite haunt of thousands of frogs, whose croaking after dark drowned out any speaker on stage, so a student would be sent to stand by the side of the pond and shine a lantern onto the water to stop their croaking.

Because education was neither free nor universal, many children started school late, as Edith had done. Sometimes the school would have to send away a child who had turned up without fees, but members of staff helped financially whenever they could. Most of the students were young adults whose country had gone through years of upheaval, and in 1969 some of the sixth form boys went on strike. They didn't like the food. They didn't like their uniforms. The teachers weren't listening to their problems. After a few ringleaders had been suspended everything settled down, but this was an indication of the way things had changed. These were young men already thinking seriously about life outside the classroom. And that included relationships.

Edith, now seventeen, was hungry to play a full part in this new world. On 27 February she went to the Scripture Union (SU) welcoming party and met the SU Secretary, David Wakumire. David opened the celebrations with a song, then someone preached, and there was tea.

It may have been SU's teaching material that spoke to Edith. The young people were told that it wasn't enough to rely on what they'd heard from their parents; each of them needed to make a personal commitment to Christ. The word that leapt out to her that day was 'salvation', a word never used in the village churches. Church-goers there were reluctant to rock a comfortable boat, much as they had been in England in the 18th century, when 'Enthusiasm' became a dirty word. (When Edith went to pray overnight at conferences later, Christine became alarmed. These people were going to ruin her sister's chances of a normal life!)

What Edith heard in St Peter's Chapel day that day changed her life forever. Now she realised that although a girl, she was made in God's image, and He was her father. Secure in that knowledge her confidence and self-esteem blossomed. Now she saw that God had always answered her prayers. She could trust him. That day Edith gave her life to the Lord.

David Wakumire, two years older than Edith, helped her to follow up that commitment. He had won a bursary by coming out in the top three in his exams. They quickly discovered how much they had in common and became good friends. Like Edith, David was fatherless. He was seven years old, the baby of the family, when his father died. His mother, Esther, had two other sons, Samson and Michael and two daughters, Angela and Mutomji. His father's second wife had four sons and a daughter. David was brought up mainly by his eldest brother, Samson. David was one of the volunteers who took turns to clean and put flowers in the chapel, and Edith gladly added her name to the roster.

David was taken by her eagerness and her frank, confident smile. Many of the school staff were young British expatriates, some with young children, and Edith soon became a popular baby-sitter.

School reports show that Edith enjoyed sports and domestic science more than the academic subjects. She was a centre player in netball and hockey, and ran the 100m, relay races and long jump for her house. She loved country dancing. Home Economics, her favourite subject, included gardening, child care, cooking and sewing. She was Prefect in the girls' hostel, and here she was particularly moved by the plight of poorer girls, helping them in practical ways. She knew how humiliating it was when you didn't even have a bar of soap to wash yourself or your underclothes.

Edith had never known a happy home with a mother's care. Now Grace Molli, the Biology and Domestic Science teacher, became a mother figure to Edith. She'd been at school with Freda, and had taught Christine. Some of the other girls whispered 'favouritism' because of Grace's mothering of Edith, but this teacher had a big heart for this young, motherless girl.

Comments in school reports include: 'Friendly, co-operative, shows courage and competence, studies diligently, neatest girl in the hostel.' Domestic Science included all the skills a girl would need to become a good wife and mother. The classroom was a model home with sitting room, bedroom, kitchen and toilet, used by twenty girls at a time. Grace taught them how to clean clothes and iron a man's trousers, how to set a table and use different fuels – electricity, gas, charcoal and firewood. Occasionally staff would be invited to sample a meal in this model home, or to purchase the cakes the girls had made. Childcare covered nutrition, preparing baby food and making milk from soya beans. Grace would either borrow a baby or use her own for demonstrations. She took the girls into her own home to show them how to make it cheerful with items they could make themselves, such as bright bedside rugs. Grace became a lifelong friend, and Edith made no major career move without her prayers and blessing. Edith's children still call Grace 'Grandma'.

The busy routine of Nabumali suited Edith. After breakfast there were prayers, and in the evening homework. After four o'clock there were sports, all played with bare feet. The six school houses played against each other, and against other schools in the district. On Sundays there was worship before lunch, free time in the afternoon, Christian Union fellowship at four o'clock and supper at seven.

Romance was soon in the air. His name was Moses. He was a good, clean-living young man, and Edith loved him, but he was impatient, eager to start adult life. He urged Edith to leave school and marry him, but she refused. She'd come so far by her own hard work and couldn't give up now. Moses wouldn't wait. Heartbroken, Edith turned to David for support about this huge disappointment, and her future.

It was mainly their fatherless state that drew the two together. Because David's half-sisters had played little part in his life, he valued girls as different, special creatures. The two made a good team, whether planning SU meetings or cleaning the chapel. In David, Edith saw the answer to those prayers of long ago, when she'd prayed 'Lord, if I must marry, let him be a Christian and a poor man, a man who values girls as human beings.' But there was one more hurdle for them to overcome – jealousy.

Edith went to a conference at another school and met a young man called Jimmy. Later his school visited Nabumali and Jimmy stayed at the school hostel. Someone mentioned him to David. When Jimmy's group were leaving, friends gathered round their bus to say their farewells. Edith introduced Jimmy to David and the two shook hands. As Jimmy climbed onto the bus he thrust some money into Edith's hand. The bus pulled away, and in her confusion Edith handed the money over to David. David threw it on the ground. Edith was astonished.

'Why did you do that?'

'Well, why did he give it to you? What had you done for him?'

'Nothing. I don't know why he gave it to me. We're just friends, that's all.'

'You took it from him because I'm poor and I've never given you anything!'

'That's not true!'

David stormed away angrily. A performance of *The Merchant of Venice* was only a few days away, and he was playing the role of the Duke. Because Edith had a small part in it he decided to drop out. It took some persuasion to convince him, first, that it was illogical to take his anger out on the play, and secondly, that he had no reason to be jealous. They talked things through. David confessed that whenever Edith gave him a small gift, he found it hard to accept: he should be the one to give. He once bought her a handkerchief and some nail polish, but even such small items meant a real financial struggle. But now they understood each other. The staff watched this attachment, saw that it was a healthy, freely-sharing friendship – but kept an eye on them all the same.

When Freda went to work in Kampala, Edith often stayed at her house during the holidays and David would visit her there. Freda loved socialising. When David saw Edith mixing with Freda's older, more sophisticated friends he became uneasy. There was always beer in the fridge. David spoke to Edith and Edith spoke to her sister. She told Freda she would no longer hand drinks out to her friends. Freda was sympathetic; from then on her guests helped themselves.

In 1969 Edith became SU Minutes Secretary for ten neighbouring schools, then Area Treasurer for Uganda SU Fellowship, which meant travelling to Mbale and Tororo. Each school held two meetings per term. She helped them plan holiday conferences, collected the money, then led sessions and discussions. As House Prefect she would listen to young girls and lonely children, especially orphan girls, and get to the root of their problems. When she saw bad behaviour she would think, 'Maybe this girl is like this because …'

Edith passed her O level exams in 1970, but her marks were not high enough to earn her a boarding place for further studies. However she'd done well in Biology and Chemistry, and because she loved farming, decided to apply for Bukalasa agricultural college. But even as she filled in the application forms Christine was thrusting another set into her hands, those for Buwalasi teacher training college. Freda and Christine used all their persuasive powers. Both their parents had been good teachers, and they felt this was where Edith's future should be. For the sake of peace, Edith sent in both applications – and both offered her a place.

Against her sisters' advice she chose agriculture. But God had other ideas. Her first week at Bukalasa was so miserable that she knew she'd made the wrong choice. By now she and David, now at Kyambogo Teachers' College, Kampala, were unofficially engaged. She needed his advice urgently, but after spending the whole week trying to get in touch with him, decided to leave Bukalasa anyway. She had one week in which to change her mind, otherwise she would lose her place at Buwalasi. Edith packed all her belongings, hired a car to take her to Kampala, and caught the Mbale bus. David, who'd gone to Mbale to see his mother, was the first person she met there. Edith told him, 'I've been looking for you: I've decided to go to Buwalasi.' David was so excited that he hired a car and took her straight there. She settled in at once and loved it.

CHAPTER 9

1971-3 ~ Idi Amin

While President Milton Obote was in Singapore in January 1971 meeting heads of other Commonwealth countries, Idi Amin, his army chief of staff, staged a coup. On 25 January thousands cheered and danced for joy in the streets of Kampala, stamping on Milton Obote's picture. Free elections were promised, up to sixty political prisoners released, and the new President announced that the body of the Kabaka, who had died in London in 1969, would be brought home for burial with full honours. President Nyerere of Tanzania called the coup 'an act of treason' but Britain recognised the new regime. The joy was shortlived. Amin was of the Kakwa tribe in the north east of Uganda. But most of his tribe were based in Zaire and the southern Sudan, with little love for Uganda. Very soon Ugandan soldiers were replaced by Kakwa, South Sudanese and Nubian mercenaries. By May there had been mass killings, six thousand in July alone.

Amin now had absolute power. But he needed help. He flew first to Israel, then to Britain asking for arms and transport, but received no help from either. Finally he tried Libya, where he was rebuffed for his links with Israel.

By the end of the year he had made up a death list of two thousand, mostly prominent people. The judge of the Uganda Supreme Court had 'disappeared'. Bodies rotted in the streets of Kampala. Day after day screams could be heard from the notorious State Research Bureau (SRB), Amin's secret police headquarters in Nakasero, Kampala. Amin's death squad targeted Acholi and Lango tribes in particular. Over the next eight years 300,000 Ugandans lost their lives. Thousands of university professors, lecturers, doctors, cabinet ministers, lawyers, business people and even military officers were dragged from their offices, shot or simply disappeared.

On 18 September 1971, Obote's supporters in exile in Tanzania, led by a young man named Yoweri Kaguta Museveni, joined Tanzanian forces to fight Amin and his regime. The attack failed, but Amin's confidence was shaken. Many Christians were attacked simply because they'd worked for or with the former government.

Freda was now working for the Permanent Secretary, the Ministry of Public Services in Cabinet Affairs at Entebbe. Before independence most of the posts had been filled by British secretaries. Now they had left and been replaced by Ugandans. Freda loved her work. In 1969 she was assigned to a delegation from the Ministry of Finance to attend World Bank meetings in Cyprus, Denmark, Sweden and Norway. Later that year she was transferred to work for the Secretary for Administration and Establishment in the President's office.

Five months after Amin took power he went on safari one day, leaving instructions that when he returned he didn't want to find his current secretary still in her post. The Acting President, Abu Mayanja, consulted his colleagues, and Freda's name was the one everyone suggested. Freda invented every possible excuse to get out of it, but the Acting President lamely suggested she make her excuses to the President in person. Idi Amin returned to find Freda behind the desk in his outer office. It was an uneasy honour. Freda had heard whispers. People only disappeared, it seemed, when Amin happened to be out of town. Occasionally she went to his Command Post at Kololo. She remembers, 'We used to hear rumours that there were skulls in the freezer there. I didn't have a reason – or the courage – to look in that freezer.' There were other difficulties. Army officers were very touchy about being addressed by their full rank. To make sure she didn't get one wrong, Freda asked a friend to draw all the distinguishing insignia for her, and kept the drawings alongside her typewriter. That way she could glance quickly at the officer's shoulder, then at the drawings, before addressing him. One speech she had to type included a mass of figures. To make sure there were no mistakes, after each figure she typed it in words in brackets. The President was furious with her for 'confusing' him. On one 'President Meets the People' tour he made a long speech in Swahili, with some fractured Luganda thrown in. Freda had to translate as he spoke, and write it all down in shorthand – in English. She was scared of him, but had no choice but to get on with her job. Some might even have envied her the glamour of flying with him to France, Italy and other countries.

The Church was a perpetual thorn in Amin's flesh. Bishop Festo Kivangere was consecrated bishop in Kampala on 5 November, but many overseas friends who had been invited were refused visas. Despite this, thousands turned up for the three-and-a-half hour service, followed by an outdoor feast of chicken, beans, bananas and soda pop. On 3 December a crowd of 11,500 turned up for his enthronement in St Paul's Cathedral, Kabale, including many of his friends from East Africa, Europe, USA and Australia. The church in Pittsburg, US, paid for his vestments.

A Christian organisation, African Enterprise, had been established in 1962 by a South African, Michael Cassidy, with branches in California, UK, Germany, Australia and South Africa. When a branch was opened in Uganda in 1971 it was felt right to distinguish it by adding the word 'Evangelical'. So it became the African Evangelistic Enterprise (AEE), with Bishop Festo Kivengere as its leader. They opened an office just below Namirembe Cathedral in Kampala.

Bishop Festo attended a conference in Dodoma, Tanzania, where President Julius Nyerere told the pastors that in his country he wanted socialism to accept God and Christ. David Wakumire says 'The Holy Spirit fell on the church in 1971. People spoke in tongues and dreamed visions, being prepared for the onslaught to come.'

In 1972 Amin broadcast to the whole of Uganda: 'I want the church to remove the words 'Zion' and 'Israel' from the bible.' The Bishops replied, 'Why broadcast to the nation? This is a church matter. Come and talk to us. Our faith is a matter of life and death.' Amin dropped the idea. But one preacher who read a psalm mentioning 'Israel' on the radio was shot. In mid-September, when World Vision sponsored the biggest ever conference of pastors in Uganda, Amin attended one of their meetings and assured them, 'You are my eyes and my right hand, and I need your advice.'

During the first week of September 1972, Amin began the destruction of Uganda's economy by expelling all of Uganda's Asians, over 70,000 people. They were given ninety days to leave the country, taking nothing with them but the clothes they wore. Strangely enough there was no looting. Their houses and shops were locked up, ready to be allocated by government decree. Cars were commandeered by the army, thousands parked at the military police depot in Mbale. Amin's cronies grabbed the vacated businesses, premises and goods. Next he nationalised British investments in tea plantations and other industries, without compensation. The economy began to collapse. There was no money to pay the army. Hospitals and rural health clinics closed. Roads started to crack. In the cities utilities fell apart. The army machine-gunned wildlife and the tourist trade evaporated. Colonel Gaddafi of Libya bailed Amin out and equipped the army with sophisticated weaponry. A boatman was hired especially to clear the corpses choking up the River Nile. Thirty Italians working on the new Owen Falls dam resigned, sickened by the daily accumulation of stinking, rotting flesh.

News of the atrocities reached Mbale. In 1972 David was about to finish his teacher training, and he cried when he saw his friends, newly-qualified Asian teachers, leaving. One of them told David, 'Our parents came from Bangladesh, but we were born here. We don't know where we'll go. Do you know anyone in government who can help us?' But David didn't. Most of them went to the United Kingdom. Many committed suicide by drowning, increasing the number of corpses floating in the Nile. There was an exodus not only of Indians, but of many well-educated Ugandans. One neighbouring priest fled to Kenya, leaving a pregnant wife. David and Edith helped her when the child was born, and when her husband returned he'd saved enough money to build a house.

Amin's illiterate or semi-literate cronies were now running the shops, with no idea where or how to obtain stocks. Even the status of marriage was affected. Well-educated woman would marry a man who was barely literate but 'shilling rich', simply because he now owned a shop or factory. Muslims who had once trusted their children's education to a Christian school now kept them there only until they could read and write, and then sent them to a Koran school to learn Arabic. The dignity of education crumbled.

In 1973, at Colonel Gaddafi's suggestion, Amin banned all Christian organisations except the Anglican, Catholic and Orthodox churches – Jehova's Witnesses, Campus Crusade for Christ, Assemblies of God, Pentecostal, The Navigators and the Full Gospel Church – and built a mosque at the entrance to Makerere University. He registered Uganda as a member of the Organisation of Islamic Conferences. All church services were spied upon.

Desmond Tutu, then a bishop in South Africa, visited Uganda in 1973. He called the country 'sad ... an overpowering sense of insecurity... People just keep disappearing and nobody knows if they will be the next on the list... The Americans have closed their Embassy because the General took umbrage at the presence of armed uniformed Marines after he had threatened to arrest the Ambassador.' The car in which Bishop Tutu was being driven by a university friend was followed by an army vehicle, and when he left his plane was held back at Entebbe for his papers and luggage to be searched.*

At the Full Gospel Church near Makerere, David's friend Obed was their Youth Pastor, and Edith's friend played the organ. Word got back to Amin that singing and dancing were still going on there, so he sent his soldiers to stop them. Although they 'fired into the air', several people were killed, their bodies dumped in the forest where a Coca Cola plant now stands. Some were captured and taken to the Nakasero underground prison. Obed survived. (The church took legal advice on choosing a new name, opening afresh at Easter 1978 as the Glad Tidings Church of Uganda. Although they had no connection with the Anglican church, they felt that the inclusion of 'Church of Uganda' gave them an air of legitimacy.)

Early in 1973 Bishop Festo phoned President Amin to complain about the arrest of three Kigizi men who were due for public execution. He went to talk to the President in person, but in vain. On 10 February a crowd of three thousand gathered to watch as the three faced a firing squad. Festo was allowed to speak to them before they died, and all three Christians died without fear. That day all over Uganda executions were held of people suspected of treason, including two young men in Mbale. By summer Amin had killed about ninety thousand.

That year John Sentamu, the twenty-four-year-old High Court Judge who would later become Archbishop of York, clashed with Amin and left for Britain. David Wakumire remembers John as a member of SU. David took a team of young people to see the play 'The City Kid', written by Edith's high school English teacher, Clive Lewis, in which John Sentamu played the main role. Later David took part in the play at Nabumali High School.

One day in February 1973 the President was away when Freda picked up the telephone. It was his Press Secretary.

'Freda? The President has asked me to give you a message. He wants you to leave the office immediately. On your way out you must hand over all your keys to his bodyguard.'

Shocked, Freda put the phone down. She gathered up her personal possessions, handed the keys over, then went home and waited. For several nights she slept under the bed, but there was no further message. Some of Amin's Cabinet Ministers were sympathetic, urging Freda to move to the East African Community Headquarters in Arusha, Tanzania. Freda refused; if the President wanted to kill her for fun, he could do it in Uganda. She wouldn't abandon her sisters who needed her financial help. One of Freda's supporters was Princess Elizabeth Bagaya, who volunteered to speak to Amin personally on Freda's behalf, and narrowly missed being kicked for her trouble. (The Princess had to flee the country, but later became Uganda's Ambassador to France.) Freda discovered that someone had told Amin that certain papers from his office had turned up in another town. Amin obviously believed it was her fault. She feared she might become one of the many 'disappeared', but to Freda's relief she was allowed to go back to teaching at the Uganda College of Commerce, where she was head of the Secretarial Department from 1973 to 1974.

But Idi Amin hadn't finished with her. One day she was having lunch at home when the telephone rang. Amin's private secretary told her to wait: the President wanted to speak to her. His voice was grim.

'This is President Idi Amin Dada. I want to talk to Filida (his name for Freda).'

'I am the one, Your Excellency.'

'I want you in my office at two o'clock. I want to give you a rocket.'

'I will be there, Your Excellency.'

Freda pushed her food away, feeling sick, and hurried to her friends nearby, warning them that if she wasn't back by the next day they should pack as many belongings they could and leave for Christine's home in Mbale.

Freda ran all the way and got there in good time. But his secretary kept her talking, and by the time she walked into his office it was past two. He was in a foul mood.

'Who do you think you are, to turn up late when summoned by a President!'

Freda apologised, and explained that sh'd been kept waiting by the secretary. Then he dropped his bombshell.

'It has been reported you're going to Tanzania to join the guerillas. Explain!'

Freda immediately suspected the 'friend' who had passed this information on to him. Disguising her anger, she stood up to him.

'Your Excellency, I'm single, and I am poor. I work hard at my job, I live alone with my children. I've never thought of going to Tanzania. I only know it from the map. But since you are the President of this nation and you have all the power, you may do whatever you want with me.'

He kept quiet for a moment, then said: 'I want to see you at State House, Entebbe, tonight.'

Freda went back to work for what was left of the day. That night a driver collected her from her home and drove her to State House. She was shown into an empty office with a solitary desk and a chair. On the desk were a typewriter, a ream of crisp white typing paper, and a huge file of handwritten notes. Nothing was said. Freda sat down and started typing. She gathered from the notes that the President planned to address the nation the following day, and this was his speech. Among the papers was a very long list of the many honours he was bestowing on himself, including that of *The Conqueror of the British Empire*. Freda worked quickly, building a neat pile of typed papers on the desk, then she went home. She spoke to no-one and heard no more from him directly.

But he still made her uneasy. Freda remembers, 'Whenever he came to the College of Commerce to officiate at the graduation ceremony, he would point me out and tell people I was his secretary! All this was after he had dismissed me from his office! A few times some of his concubines came to attend a secretarial course and I was worried what could happen to me if they did not perform well enough to pass the set examinations. Luckily enough they performed well and passed on merit.'

Edith suspected that her sister's situation could be dangerous, but was spared the full details until much later.

In 1975 Freda started work as secretary to the Vice President and Minister of Defence, Paulo Mwanga, in Kampala. He, too, was feared by many, especially the Baganda because of their connections with Obote. Friends were alarmed and asked Freda, 'How dare you go there? You're dead!' But Freda found him fair, although assertive. He was even soft-hearted on occasion. When suspects were brought in from the bush during the civil war, he would send Freda out to get food and drink for them. With the Vice President, Freda flew in a military plane to North Korea twice and had dinner with the Great Leader. With the Prime Minister she flew to twenty different countries, including Germany, Moscow, India, China, Cyprus, Greece, Ethiopia, Egypt, Scotland and Wales. She filled this post for four years.

Rabble Rouser for Peace p130

CHAPTER 10

1973-7 ~ marriage, a baby, and university

During Edith's two years at Buwalasi, David was still at Kyambogo. He had overcome his natural shyness and became very popular with the girls. Perhaps his guitar-playing was part of the attraction. A photograph of Edith very prominently displayed in his room discouraged any other would-be girlfriends.

A qualified teacher at last, Edith joined the staff of Nyondo Demonstration School, where she would teach for three years. She was given a house near the Convent at Nyondo, and would walk two miles every day to Nabumali for her teaching practice. Every day she stopped for lunch and a rest at the home of Sophie and John Watulo, who had both trained in Australia. Sophie was a Senior Tutor at the college. Later Edith moved in with them for a whole year. She was still there when she and David were married in 1974. That year David was posted to Nabumali High School, where he was allocated a big house.

With her first pay packet Edith rushed out and bought two lengths of dress material for Aunt Soferesi. From the day Edith became a Christian she'd prayed that she might love her aunt. She'd worked so hard for this, and chose a blue flowered fabric carefully. Edith presented the parcel to her aunt and waited eagerly as the old fingers unwrapped the brown paper. Soferesi fingered the material, then sniffed, 'I don't like the colour.' Ashamed, Edith apologised. 'I'm sorry, I thought you'd like it. But it doesn't matter. Take it anyway, and I'll choose another colour.' She went back to the factory the next day, chose a dress length in a different colour, and had a dress made for her aunt. Soferesi kept the first two lengths, but never thanked Edith for either them or the dress.

David and Edith wanted a formal engagement, but there were hurdles to overcome.

An engagement ceremony is known as the 'Introduction, when a woman must present her man formally to her family, and the men negotiate important details such as the date of the wedding and the bride price. The bulk of the dowry, usually cows, goes to the men. Any perishables left after the men have taken their pick are shared among the women. Once the dowry is paid, the woman is regarded as bought property. If a marriage fails, it must be paid back. Clearly nobody wants this to happen. Instead the disappointed husband and his male relatives send the woman back to her family as 'useless'. Her family can't afford to repay the dowry so she's usually thrown out. Women suffer greatly from this insecurity.

Edith didn't want to be in this position. She told Freda and Christine, 'If God lets me get married I don't want the bride price to be paid for me.'

They knew that Edith had nothing to be ashamed of in her relationship with David; this would be a Christian marriage. But there was another delicate issue: by tradition the youngest sister should not marry before her older sisters. Neither Freda nor Christine had been married formally.

Freda said, 'Don't worry, we're on your side and we won't stop you. Why don't you talk to Uncle Micah? He's a good man, and he'll help you. Make an appointment to see him.'

Uncle Micah, their father's half-brother, was an army man, a highly-respected member of the clan. Edith had always been scared of him and kept her distance, but Freda knew he had many of their father's sympathetic qualities. Edith was nervous when she turned up with David on the appointed day. She knew he liked a drink, but that day he was sober. He shook hands solemnly with David. Edith asked if he could help them.

Uncle Micah smiled, flattered that the young couple had sought his help.

'What can I do to help?'

Edith told him that the clan were asking David for a bride price. She explained her strong feelings about this, and that her sisters were on her side.

Uncle Micah was quiet for a while, then said, 'Muduwa, I'm glad you've come to me, but I don't have time to chase people around, so if they want me to take part they must do as I suggest. If David has any gifts at all, we'll be happy to accept them.'

He arranged the Introduction for a date in August 1973. David scraped up enough money to buy a few presents. Aunt Soferesi asked for a blanket and some paraffin. There were a few other token gifts, but no cash or cows. Some of the uncles cursed quietly, but they had no choice but to agree. Uncle Micah was the couple's friend for life. Years later when he was ill David bought him a coat and long white robe, the *kanzu*. He wept: none of his children had ever bought him such a gift.

The Introduction was progressing slowly, but there was one last hurdle to overcome. According to tradition, once an engagement is confirmed, a young couple are at liberty to live together. Why didn't David and Edith move into a family house that happened to be vacant? When the two insisted they had no intention of living or sleeping together until after the wedding, there was some scornful muttering, but they'd set their feet firmly on the path of a Christian marriage. Nothing would break that resolve.

By 1974 the effects of political upheaval, including the expulsion of the Asians, had left the country short of every commodity. Most shops had been taken over by Nubians, Muslims, soldiers, and wives of Amin's friends, who had no idea how to run a business or where to acquire stock. Prices rocketed. The Ministry of Commerce & Industry had to allocate essentials to schools and government offices at lower prices. In early 1974 a whisper would spread that a certain shop had sugar, tea, oil, salt, soap or bananas, and long queues would form. As the shelves emptied, Christians were pushed aside, and any *Hajat* (Muslim pilgrim) brought to the front of the queue. Some Christians made life easier by converting to Islam. The huge, flourishing sugar factory at Jinja ground to a halt and Amin started importing sugar from Cuba.

The clan wanted time to save for a big wedding party, and suggested waiting a year. David and Edith were adamant: they had already booked St Peter's chapel at Nabumali High School for 4 May 1974.

Long before the wedding friends would join any queue to buy small amounts of dried fruit and sugar, handing them over to Grace Molli for the cake. When they had enough, Grace and Edith baked and iced it in the school kitchen. David's family bought them a mattress, some bedding and a few small items.

The chapel was booked, the invitations sent out, and everything prepared. But when David's eldest brother, Samson, was rushed into hospital two days before their big day the clan shouted, 'Stop the wedding!' A wedding is above all traditionally a time for rejoicing. There was a real danger that if Samson died or was on his death-bed on the wedding day, the villagers would stone the couple as they walked from the church to the marriage feast. The wedding must be postponed either until Samson recovered, or for a year after his death. David was in a dilemma: strictly speaking he couldn't marry without his brother's permission. It was Samson who'd sent out the wedding invitations, as a father would have done. When David's father had died, Samson, then a college tutor, had been engaged to Jessica, but put off his wedding to take the seven-year-old boy and his fatherless siblings into his home. He had told Jessica, 'If you marry me, you'll have to take these children as well.' Jessica married him, and became a mother to them all. Samson had always encouraged the couple to take joint responsibility as they planned their life together.

So David rushed to the hospital just as Samson was about to be wheeled into the operating theatre. He asked what he should do. Samson knew that postponing the wedding would cause them a financial crisis. But most important, he knew that if he died, David would take responsibility for his widow and five children. Faced with that burden, David would never be able to save for another wedding. With a quiet chuckle Samson put his brother's mind at rest. 'Go ahead with the wedding. Get married first, then come and bury me later.' David prayed with his brother and said goodbye, then watched as they wheeled him away.

David told the family what Samson had said. To him and Edith, marriage wasn't simply a cause for rejoicing, but a serious commitment. With Samson's blessing, they could now stand firm against the family.

The wedding was all they had hoped for. Christian friends brought gifts of food and money. Edith's friend Betty Wafula gave Edith a wedding dress, and Freda, Matron of Honour, found the rest of her clothes. Grace Molli took the place of Mother of the Bride. Freda's daughter Joanne and Margaret's daughter Mary were bridesmaids. In Edith's words, 'It was the simplest wedding you could think of compared to other weddings at the time.' For the meal in the school dining room her sisters bought bottled sodas for the high table, but plain fruit juice for the others. As soon as the meal was finished Edith changed from her wedding dress and the couple drove to the hospital.

The newly-weds spent their wedding night waiting in a hospital corridor. By now Samson was in intensive care. When they were allowed to see him the next morning, he couldn't speak. But when they showed him their wedding rings, he smiled and nodded. He died two days later. At once David and Edith took care of Jessica and her five children.

With David teaching at Nabumali and Edith at Nyondo Demonstration School there was no honeymoon for the newlyweds. They bought land and built a house nearby for David's mother. They already had the responsibility of Samson's family, and two months after the wedding Edith became pregnant. And before the year was out they had acquired the first of seven foster children.

Stephen Watiti was David's teenage nephew. When Stephen became a Christian his parents threw him out of the house. Going to church on Sundays was one thing; being 'born again' was another. It wasn't normal. The newly-weds welcomed him into their home. Stephen always joked that he was their firstborn.

When Edith was in her sixth month of pregnancy David started buying things for the baby: dried milk, teething rings, a toy butterfly and helicopter. He was so excited that anything would do. On 5 April 1975 Edith's contractions started. David rushed her to Mbale hospital then hurried back to work. He stayed at home that night, returning to school the following morning, still with no news. David was on his way to teach a chemistry class when he was called to the phone. It was a tired but excited Edith. 'Solomon has come!' (Naturally David's firstborn son had to be called Solomon.) David ran to the Headmaster, who said he could go, but first he must give the class something to do. Quickly, David set some tests and rushed to the hospital. He kissed Edith's beaming face, examined the baby, confirmed that everything was in good order, then picked up his baby son and danced around the ward with him. Later that day Edith went home, and David cooked a meal for her. The following morning David was back at work, marking those tests he'd set the day before. Solomon was a fine, healthy boy. They hadn't been married a full year, but they already had two sons, plus Jessica and her five children. `

Motherhood was important to Edith, but she also had her work. Edith and David had prayed from the beginning that God would help them to do something to show appreciation for what He'd done for them. They set out together to share the word of God in schools, and to counsel students struggling with problems. At Nyondo Edith became Senior Teacher. She understood the problems of female students from the very gravest down to the humiliation of not being able to afford a bar of soap. She taught them that they were beautiful, made in God's image and valued by Him as girls and women. Edith started Home Economics classes, led MU groups in Nabumali Parish, then became the MU Archdeaconry Link Secretary. Her mother had been a member Of MU, and she knew what an important organisation it was. Out in the villages illiteracy was an ever-present problem, and much teaching, for instance the rearing of chickens, had to be done from scratch. But the main aim of MU was (and is) to keep families strong. When Muslims came to them for help they were never turned away. Whatever the creed, the needs were the same.

Sophie Watoolo, another tutor, became a mother figure to Edith during these early years of her marriage, teaching Edith much that was to prove valuable later in life. Sophie taught her, 'Girls must be taught to concentrate on their education: there's time for love and leisure later. And don't give a male teacher sexual favours just to get higher marks. If you know he's deliberately under-marked for that reason, you must report him.'

Laughing, teasing and teaching came naturally to Sophie and her husband John. Sophie told Edith: 'Your husband is your first born.' John joked with David: 'You may be head of the family, but Edith is the neck.'

The couple could have settled down to teaching and raising their family, but David Wakumire knew that his wife was capable of far more. And he realised that to go further she needed higher qualifications.

David presented her with the application forms for Makerere University to obtain a Diploma of Education, and volunteered to care for the children while she studied.

In March 1976 a student was shot dead by Amin's men outside the Makerere campus. Edith was five months pregnant when she was called for an interview in early April. An official enquiry into the March killing fizzled out, but in June a principal witness was pulled from her office and shot dead. When students held a protest demonstration on 3 August, Amin's thugs stormed the halls of residence and arrested over two hundred, including the daughter of Bishop Festo Kivengere, beating them with spiked clubs, and throwing them into prison. The jailed students were released, but men in another hall of residence were attacked so viciously that some were crippled for life.

Tamar was born on 11 August.

In December 1976 David was the East Ugandan delegate at a big crusade at the Kenyatta International Conference Centre in Nairobi, when John Stott and Billy Graham were the speakers. Friends from South Africa were there. David had the opportunity of a heart-to-heart talk with Archbishop Janani Luwum of Uganda, who had been booked to make this an international event. David urged him to use this conference as a sounding board against both apartheid and Amin. But the Archbishop told David about the battle he'd had with Amin: he was convinced that if they used this conference to air their views they wouldn't survive back home. At David's invitation the Archbishop visited Nabumali High School in January 1977.

On that trip to Nairobi, David bought Stephen his first pair of shoes. Stephen had been a great blessing to them, always happy to help with the housework or to feed and bathe the younger children. The boy was clearly heading for university. And you couldn't buy a pair of decent shoes in Uganda. So David measured the length of Stephen's feet and chose the shoes carefully. Stephen was both proud and grateful. But it hadn't occurred to David to measure the width, and Stephen didn't pluck up courage to confess there was a problem until he'd endured weeks of torture.

Edith joined Makerere University in January 1977, the start of an uneasy year. Although she was aware of all the disturbances there the year before, she was determined to stick to her plans. She knew it was God's will for her to seek further qualifications, and she'd never achieved anything except against great odds. But she had other things to worry about, like leaving a toddler and new baby in someone else's care.

CHAPTER 11

1977-80 ~ a country in turmoil, and a growing family

The East African Community broke down in 1977. Kenya, Tanzania and Uganda were by now independent nations, and the system of mutual reliance that had worked well for years ceased to exist. Each country now had its own currency. The shared transport system of railways and lake services, which had run from the borders of Mozambique, Malawi and Zambia in the south right up to the Sudan in the north, was split between the three. As a consequence Uganda's crops of coffee and cotton could no longer be carried by ferry across Lake Victoria. Whatever little produce was left now had to be carried by ill-maintained lorries along hundreds of miles of rapidly disintegrating roads.

The Church Missionary Society had reached Uganda on 30 June 1877, and plans had long been in place for centenary celebrations to be held in Kampala in 1977. Dignitaries from all over the world had been invited. But Idi Amin was uneasy. The church had played too important a part for his liking. It had created schools and hospitals as well as churches.

In January that year the House of Bishops gathered in Kampala to protest publicly against the mass killings. Thousands of innocent people were being tortured and killed. They presented a plea to the President, there in full military uniform, to respect human rights.

On 30 January, Archbishop Luwum joined nearly 30,000 for the consecration of Bishop Bamunoba of West Ankole. The bible reading for that day was from Acts 20:22-28: *'I am not scared of these dangers, for my life is no longer of any value to me myself except that I may fulfil the ministry I have received to witness to the grace of God.'* In his sermon, Bishop Festo Kivengere challenged first the bishops, and then the many dignitaries present, including intelligence officers and the President's representative. To the bishops he said:

'Therefore, guard, watch over, plead for the church which He bought. It is the preciousness of the soul that makes the minister valuable.'

Then to the government authorities:

'Many of you have misused your authority, taking things by force, using too much force. Jesus Christ used His authority to save men and women – how are you using your authority? If you misuse the authority God gave you, God is going to judge you, because He is the One who gave it to you.'[1]

Amin had good reason to be nervous. News had been suppressed that only five days earlier, while he had celebrated the anniversary of his coup by distributing 2,000 medals, there had been an attempted army coup against him.

Few people present that day ever saw Archbishop Luwum again.

There was shooting in broad daylight in the streets of Kampala on 1 February.

On 16 February the Archbishop was arrested and killed, and with him Erinayo Wilson Oryema, Minister of Land, Housing and Physical Planning and Charles Oboth-Ofumbi, Internal Affairs Minister. The story of this crime, disguised at the time as a car accident, is common knowledge and well-documented. The BBC announced starkly that the Archbishop had been murdered. Speaking on the telephone to his Attorney General, Amin laughed, 'God has given them their punishment.'[2] Many of the clergy fled. Bishop Festo Kivengere escaped to Rwanda with his wife, and later wrote of his experiences. Several bishops fled to Kenya. The Archbishop's family home had been searched for hidden weapons after dark one night the previous November, and the President had been incensed by Archbishop Luwum's firm stand.

A grave was prepared for the Archbishop's body, and a funeral planned for Sunday 20 February at Namirembe Cathedral cemetery, but where was the body? Enquirers at the heavily-guarded mortuary in Mulago hospital were told that all three bodies had already been buried in their home towns. What started as a murmur among Ugandan

Christians grew to a roar and spread around the world.

Edith was in Kampala that Sunday. The atmosphere was uneasy. Although they knew that Amin's mercenary thugs would try to stop them, hundreds of Makerere students, Edith among them, stepped out for Namirembe cathedral, determined to honour their dead Archbishop. Amin's men were everywhere, but could only watch as thousands filled the streets. Many overseas friends who'd been invited to the funeral were refused visas, but four-and-a-half thousand Christians defied government threats and set off for the cathedral. As they marched they sang over and over again the song first sung by the young martyrs in 1885: 'Glory, glory, halleluiah, Glory to the Lamb.' The whisper grew, 'Where is the body?' Many saw an eerie similarity between the Archbishop's death and that of Jesus – a funeral with no body, Retired Archbishop Erica Sabiti took as the theme for his sermon that day the words of the angel that first Easter Sunday: 'He is not here. He is risen!'

Members of MU marched through the streets in their distinctive uniform – the traditional *gomas* in white with a bright blue sash. Many men wore the formal long white *kanzu*, ready for martyrdom, if that was how the day should end. From that day people became more open about spreading the gospel. They had been in hiding, many wearing caps like Muslims, but now they came out prepared for battle.

Amin had always been particularly venomous towards the Acholi and Langi tribes, and between February and May about 10,000 of them were arrested and slaughtered. Six young actors preparing a play about the early martyrs for the centenary celebrations were murdered, their bodies dumped in a field outside Kampala.

Bishop Festo Kivengere said of Idi Amin:

'In my view he is a military man who has tried to rule with too much force, and in doing so has himself become a victim of that force. He has created machinery that it has become impossible for him to control.'

Amin became fanatical about all things connected with Israel. He closed the Israeli Embassy, kicking out all Israelis who were working on the new Entebbe airport and Lumumba Hall. He even made it a crime to go on pilgrimage to Jerusalem.

Other, more practical problems for Christians led to much

conscience-searching. The black market had become a way of life. There was now a world embargo on Ugandan coffee, and Amin was selling it for foreign currency to buy guns. Producers could no longer market their cotton or coffee legitimately. The problem came to a peak in 1977, when growers, David's sister among them, had a two-year stock of unsold coffee beans. Thousands of people packed their coffee into kerosene tins and trudged through the night with it on their heads, over the mountain into Kenya. It was a dangerous trade and many lost their lives. Amin's soldiers carried out large-scale smuggling in lorries, and would shoot to kill any 'competition', stealing their coffee. Smugglers were also challenged by hostile tribes with spears. In Kenya the coffee would be bartered for blankets, sugar, salt, kerosene and fat on a large scale. Kenya would market the high quality coffee as its own produce. 'Buy cheap and sell dear' was their motto. When thriving companies like African Textile Mills and Nytil Cotton closed down, second-hand clothing became big business.

David's school was among the many affected. Pupils would join caravans Arab style, coffee on their heads, *askaris* fore and aft. One of David's brightest students handed in his text books; he was going coffee-carrying. In one school a pupil from a rich family even employed his teacher to carry their coffee. Soldiers searching for contraband approached one family, noticed a very large pot and asked what was in it. The family assured them it was being used as a beehive. In disbelief, the men broke the pot and the family laughed as they fled, screaming, to escape the angry swarm.

There was another problem, a moral one. David was responsible for buying necessities such as soap for the school, the children's programmes and youth camps. He had to choose: queue for whatever was available in the shops at ever-rocketing prices, or buy black market. He decided to stay legal, and went to draw some cash from the bank. The teller knew David, and raised his eyebrows when he saw the size of the cheque.

'I know it's not my business, but out of curiosity, why do you need so much cash?'

David told him. The teller laughed. 'Soap? You must be crazy! Spend all this on a few bars of soap? Tell you what, I'll tear up this cheque, then you just take a bit of cash and buy black market. That's what anybody else would do.'

David found a way round the problem that tied in with his Christian ideals. Amin had banned the sale of all Christian publications in Uganda, including bibles and music tapes. Open Doors, founded by Brother Andrew, were already distributing bibles and Christian literature in Romania and Russia, both under a Communist regime. When he heard of the oppression in Uganda Brother Andrew made several visits as a tourist, and realising that its people were suffering as much as those in Communist countries, he opened a base in Nairobi. David volunteered for this work and organised an underground church in his home linked with Open Doors. He carried out this work in Eastern Uganda until 1984. Trained by Open Doors in the art of 'crossing the border', he would set off for Kisumu on the shores of Lake Victoria, a short distance across the border with Kenya, leaving his car on the Uganda side. He would collect books from a publishing house near Kisumu, pushing them over the border in a wooden hand cart. One day the border guards near Busia stopped him.

'What's that you're carrying?'

'Tracts for encouragement.'

'Don't you know that religion is banned?'

'Yes, but Jesus isn't banned. Just read it.'

That day he went home empty-handed, but convinced that he had left the tracts where they were most needed.

While he was in Kenya he could buy goods from Nairobi and Kisumu, not only books but second-hand clothes and baby things for Solomon and Tamar. And lots of soap.

David was only once afraid for his life. He was driving in Kampala when two soldiers stopped him, forced him out of the car at gunpoint, took his car keys, wallet and watch, then opened the boot of the car. There was nothing in it of any importance, and only a little cash in the wallet. They rattled questions at him: where had he been, where was he going, and why? David realised that because his car had Kenya number plates they'd assumed he must be carrying black market goods from Kenya. But there was no sign of either goods or money. He was just a working man going home. To his astonishment and relief they gave him back the car keys and let him go – but they kept the watch and wallet.

Edith's first year at Makere was a struggle. David brought his mother to the house to take care of the children, but she had her hands full with Solomon, so they found a young woman to care for baby Tamar. During the long vacation at the end of June, Edith began to suspect that Tamar wasn't thriving as she should. At first David tried to brush her fears aside. The child was a little slow, but she was plump enough. But Edith was uneasy; her first baby had been full of life, this one was listless. They took Tamar to a doctor, and were shocked when he told them she was showing the first signs of Kwashikor. They discovered that the babysitter had been watering down the baby's milk and pocketing the money she'd saved. Edith used the long vacation to bring baby Tamar back to health, playing with her and giving her nourishing food. It didn't take long for them to find a new babysitter, or for Tamar to start bouncing as babies should. Edith said later: 'I would have lost my only daughter for the sake of studies. Thank God that long vacation happened in time to rescue her.'

In 1978 Amin declared that Friday was to be a public holiday. For many this meant that Uganda now had a three day weekend, but schools taught on Saturdays instead of Friday, with four lessons crammed into the morning.

That year Edith had an internship and stayed at Ksabwangasi Teachers' College for one year. Solomon and Tamar stayed with her. On 15 February she gave birth to Samson Abbednego Watulutsu in Kampala. She joked that she got a baby instead of a diploma, but this didn't hold her back for very long.

When David was invited to the Love Africa Conference to be held in the Central African Republic, he was refused permission by the Department of Religious Affairs, part of Amin's Ministry of Internal Affairs. The word 'congress' had appeared somewhere in their literature, stirring up memories of Obote's Uganda People's Congress.

Instead, in August David organised a week's youth conference in Mbale. They were closely watched by members of the SRB. Four out of five of those attending were Muslims. When David showed the *Jesus* film many Muslims came to see it, and many came to know the Lord. On the last day, Sunday, David had invited a speaker, and decided to end the week with an open air gathering around a camp fire. As they strode up the mountainside, word got back to Kampala that they were going for guerrilla training. A Volkswagen car with an official from the SRB was waiting for them when they came back down. David showed him their programme for the day and talked about prayer. Nothing more was said.

David's stepbrother, Samuel, was a taxi driver. There was a good trade in spare parts, and when an SRB officer commandeered Samuel's vehicle, David complained to the Regional Police Commissioner. An appointment was made for him to meet the SRB officer at Police headquarters. David told him, 'You can keep the car, but make sure my brother doesn't get into any trouble.' The matter was smoothed over, and Samuel recovered his car from the military barracks. It was clear to David that there was no love lost between the Police and the SRB.

In school, David was now SU Representative and Assistant Chaplain. SU conferences became known as 'life-changing'. For the first time, Nubian students were being enrolled at the school, and were very persistent in attending chapel. Everyone knew they were spies. David believes he heard God telling him in a dream, 'My voice is becoming faint.' Against the Headmaster's advice, he held a conference for brethren from the banned churches. When he travelled to Kenya for Open Doors, friends there tried to persuade him to move to Kenya. They needed qualified Biology, Chemistry and Physics teachers, and David would be safe there. But there were three good reasons for not leaving. Firstly, he would lose the house and property for which he'd worked so hard. Secondly, Edith would have to abandon her training course. Finally, he had to stand firm with his family and students.

That November the Headmaster at David's school was warned that the SRB were coming to get the Head of Chemistry. Quickly, the Head sent the office boy, to warn him. He escaped. David went to Kampala in his place to get the chemicals and equipment for the approaching exams.

The SRB had special radios for passing any information directly on to Amin. David often used to see them around Mbale. If they saw two people talking for a while they'd stroll up and listen. You could see that people were living in fear.

When Tanzania invaded Uganda on 30 October 1978, Yoweri Museveni took part in the war of liberation. Uganda bombed the Lake

Victoria ports of Bukoba and Musoma in North West Tanzania.

At 10 p.m. on 22 January 1979 in a Radio Uganda broadcast from Dar es Salaam, Milton Obote urged the population of Uganda to rise up. Nyerere had scraped together a 50,000 army and counter-attacked. By the end of April his army had taken Kampala. Amin fled to Libya. (In 2004 he died in Saudi Arabia, where his body remained.) The cost of the war to Tanzania was enormous. Unpaid soldiers, left behind, went on the rampage, looting, hijacking and slaughtering wildlife. Armed bandits roamed the cities, food supplies ran out and hospitals could no longer function. A three-year drought had brought about severe famine, especially in the North, and the AEE organised relief, with a programme for feeding hoards of school children.

With Amin gone, thousands of exiled Ugandans began to return. Yusuf Lule, one time Principal of Makerere University, took over as President, appointed by a consultative meeting of Uganda National Liberation Front in Moshi, Tanzania. But when he spoke out against Nyerere he was replaced by Godfrey Binaisa. Lule's supporters sparked off riots in Kampala. Obote had been waiting for this, the moment for his return. Binaisa reluctantly set a date for a general election, but it was blatantly rigged in Obote's favour, and Binaisa was exiled to the USA. It is estimated that 300,000 Ugandans were killed during Amin's reign of terror, but at last there was some prospect of peace.

On 23 December 1979 the fourth and last Wakumire baby, Christopher, was born. In 1980 Edith completed her training at Makerere University and went to Nyondo Teachers' College for ten years. As Senior Tutor she started Home Economics classes, and led MU groups in church.

Edith's doctor had advised her that gor her health's sake there should be no more babies. When Edith broached the subject of family planning, David was against it. He was not alone. Men see a large family as a sign of strength: even when a man agrees, he leaves his wife to do what's necessary. At first David felt the concept was against his Christian beliefs. And neither of them was familiar with the practicalities.

But David listened at last. Even so, he was determined that any advice must be from a Christian doctor. They located Dr Ejumu Moses in Ngora hospital, to the north west of Mbale. Patiently Dr Moses explained the advantages of family planning and the different methods available. A few weeks later Edith was fitted with a coil. The family continued to grow, but there were no more babies.

Three family events took place in 1980. At ten o'clock one Saturday morning Christine accepted the Christian faith. And Uncle Micah died. Edith couldn't stay for his burial because baby Christopher had the measles and nearly died in hospital that day, but she said her own farewell to Micah as he lay in his coffin.

Then something happened to five-year-old Solomon that cast a long, dark shadow over the family.

[1] *I Love Idi Amin* p44
[2] *A State of Blood* p188

CHAPTER 12

1980-5 ~ Solomon's eye, David's outreach

Well, what else was a feisty five-year-old supposed to do? When another boy dares you to open the gate of the piggery, you open it. The gate's fastened with a twisted wire, but that's OK. You can untwist it. Like this.

Solomon untwisted the wire, the end sprung back and cut his eye. David was away at the time. Because of the war Edith could find neither transport nor petrol, and the nearest help was at Nyondo Catholic Dispensary. All they could do was to give him painkillers. When David arrived home a week later they managed to get a lift to Mbale hospital, where he was given eye drops. A month later the eye was no better. Solomon cried all the time, covering his eyes with his hands. In desperation David and Edith contacted the Flying Doctor Service at Ngora. It took the doctor only a moment to confirm that the eye was seriously damaged and a traumatic cataract was forming. He offered to fly Solomon to Mulago Hospital in Kampala, but they would have to pay all medical expenses. David wasn't happy about this. Apart from the cost, the medical facilities in Uganda were in a deplorable state, even at what had not long ago been a new, prestigious teaching hospital. There were only about 550 doctors for the whole population of 15.2m. A second opinion recommended sending Solomon to Nairobi, so David took him there by bus – a two day journey – while Edith stayed at home with the other children. Despite the appalling cost of three weeks in hospital, it was now too late to save the eye. Painkillers were the only help for the five-year-old.

Solomon became shy and withdrawn. Aunt Soferesi didn't help by calling him 'handicapped' – and even worse. At school reading was a struggle, and the other children teased him. Increasingly reluctant to leave the home compound, he was happy to be left alone to clean the house, like his 'big brother' Stephen. Solomon became a good cook, his speciality chapattis.

By 1981 David recognised that that there were huge numbers of damaged, suffering children needing more than education. The wars in the North had left thousands dead or homeless. Mass graves were unearthed. Obote had favoured the northern tribes and established a secret security organ similar to Amin's SRB. Prisons were filling up once again, the press were muzzled and western journalists expelled. David gave up teaching, and on 1 January 1981 joined the African Evangelical Enterprise (AEE). On their behalf he travelled to cities in Africa and Europe, preaching in churches, schools and refugee camps. His was a 'words *and* deeds' ministry. He shared the gospel through feeding programmes and youth camps, issues ignored by the church. Very soon David and his stepbrother, Samuel, had formed the Christian Fellowship Outreach, with two aims: firstly to trace relatives of these children, secondly to find sponsorship for their care and education. In normal times orphaned children were easily absorbed into the extended family. But these were not normal times. Many lost children simply didn't know who they were. (Even now, twenty years later, although registration of births and deaths is required by law, only 4% are registered, and only 1% of the population has a birth certificate.) This work formed the roots of the work both David and Edith are involved in today.

In 1983 David made his first trip to Europe to promote his children's programme in the UK. He reached England in time to enjoy Spring Harvest, then caught the Harwich/Hook of Holland ferry for Amsterdam. Four thousand delegates from all over the world were there for the Billy Graham conference, and David represented AEE. Billy Graham had wanted 70% of the places to be filled with men from developing countries, preferably under the age of thirty-five, so David was just the man. Flags of 132 nations were flown at the opening ceremony. Evangelists were given gifts including cassette players. The evangelist Reinhard Bonke told the African delegates that he planned to hold a 'Fire Conference' for African evangelists in Zimbabwe in April 1986.

Samuel was with David on that visit, and in England they preached together at churches in the Garstang area, Lancashire. They told the congregations about their mission with orphaned children, especially those orphaned as a result of the atrocities of Amin's army.

At Garstang David met Elizabeth Swarbrick, who had been a midwife and teacher in the Teso District of Uganda, one of the many driven away by the Amin regime. She returned to Uganda in 1988 to help with their sponsorship work, and her friendship was to have a lasting impact on the family.

David founded the Christian Childcare Project (CCP) in Mbale in 1984. Through this ministry thousands of children, mainly orphans, received education and found work. David said, 'You get satisfaction that you have at least given a hand to help someone else who was like you.'

In January 1985 Edith was trained for chaplaincy at the Bishop Tucker Theological College, Mukono.

Edith had no more babies after 1979, but the house kept filling with foster children. The word 'No' just wasn't part of David and Edith's vocabulary. After the death of Edith's cousin Abednigo, his fifth wife came to David and Edith with her two boys. Her father's death had left her sick and penniless in a large, polygamous family. Seventeen-year-old Lawrence stayed with his mother, but fifteen-year-old Paul, who became very attached to David and Edith, moved in with them. CCP helped both the boys to complete their education. When his mother died Paul said, 'We've lost our father and mother, but we don't feel like orphans.'

In 1985 David's sister Angela and her three daughters moved into their home. Multiple marriage, widowhood and remarriage had left her and her girls homeless. Their house was burnt down. The co-wife threatened to kill her and her 'worse than useless' daughters. They escaped, but on reaching Mbale all had to be hospitalised with malaria. David built a house for Angela. Her two eldest daughters, Alice and Leah, moved in with David's mother, but nine-year-old Janet joined the Wakumire family as foster-daughter. Only when she was able to earn her own living did she leave their home.

Angela had two more daughters from her first marriage. One of them, Lois, had a daughter called Esther Nilly, born in 1974 and named after David's mother. An aunt took Esther into her home at Mukono. In early 1986 the civil war was in its final stages, but there were still threats of rioting, killing and house-burning. Life was especially dangerous for a girl approaching puberty, and twelve-year-old Esther was kept away from school. She remembers, 'When you heard a whistle you knew the rebels were coming. Auntie would whisper, "Into the bush, quick, and don't make a noise". Even the bush was scary, with snakes and wild animals, but we were more scared of the war.'

When David and Edith built their new house, Esther moved in with them and David provided for her education through CCP. Esther's own experience gave her an insight into the plight of the children who later came into her care through Edith's work. She became a source of strength to the whole family.

Then there was four-year-old Joy, the youngest of seven orphans in Edith's extended family. For eight years they paid for her education and treated her as their own before she went to live with her brothers and sisters. Later Jonathan, David's teenage nephew came under their roof, and stayed on.

That March David flew to Monrovia in Liberia with AEE, an opportunity to bring things back for the family that were still in short supply, such as material for school uniforms.

David and Edith were overjoyed when Stephen Watiti brought his fiancée, Margaret, a bank clerk, to be married from their home. They had always regarded Stephen, now a fully-qualified doctor, as their eldest son. After their wedding at Mbale Cathedral, the wedding feast was a simple affair of fruit juice, bananas, popcorn and peanuts, but for the high table David and Edith crossed the border into Kenya to buy bottled soda.

In mid 1985 Milton Obote was overthrown in a coup staged by the army under the command of Tito Okello. A 20,000 strong guerrilla army, the National Resistance Army, opposed to Obote's tribally-biased government, was massing in western Uganda. Their leader, Yoweri Museveni, had been exiled in Tanzania during Amin's reign. But Obote had muzzled the press, and few people knew that this guerrilla army was largely made up of teenage orphans. Discipline was tough. New recruits were told that they must be servants of the people, not their oppressors. People identified with the persecuted Baganda in the infamous Luwero Triangle, north of Kampala. This was an area of dense bush and forest, an ideal base for guerrilla activities. Museveni wanted a clean sweep and an end to corruption, with all those responsible for atrocities under Amin and Obote brought to trial. By now corruption was rife, with Okello responsible for more atrocities. The fighting continued.

Their old friend Phenehas came to see David one day in 1985.

'I've heard some strange rumours, David. People around here are saying that you and Edith aren't Christians any more.'

'Not Christians? Whatever do they mean?'

Phenehas kept his face straight. 'They've heard you playing the guitar and Edith singing: that's what people do in pubs. So you must have gone astray and joined some strange sect.'

David laughed. 'Next time you hear that rumour, ask if they've ever heard what another David said: "Praise him with stringed instruments, let everything that hath breath praise the Lord!"'

Yes, their small home, always full of visitors and people in need, was also full of song.

CHAPTER 13

1985-7 ~ AIDS and Singapore

In January 1986 the National Resistance Army forced the surrender of 1,600 government soldiers holed up in barracks in Mbarara, and reached Kampala. Shooting could be heard from many office blocks. Okello's troups put up little resistance and fled, commandeering vehicles and looting until they were finally pushed over the border into Sudan.

Needing bigger premises, the AEE bought the building in Kampala which had once been Amin's notorious SRB headquarters. Bloodstained cellars, once torture chambers, were scrubbed clean. Now they were used to store Christian literature, as well as 'care parcels' of soap, dried milk and clothing sent by German supporters. Bishop Festo said, 'From being a house of death, this has been turned into a house for life.' *

But now there was another war going on in Uganda, this time against an invisible enemy. After years of political upheaval and deprivation the general health of the population was poor. Even so, young people should not have been dying in large numbers as they were from malaria, tuberculosis and cancer. At first this new killer disease was known as 'Slim', because a common symptom was the loss of weight. It was killing the young, productive section of the population, leaving thousands of orphans with only elderly relatives to take care of them. AIDS first appeared in Uganda in 1982 in the Rakai district, near the western shores of Lake Victoria and the border with Tanzania. It had reached the Mbale region by 1985.

When it was recognised that AIDS was commonly passed on by promiscuous behaviour, there was in some communities a moralistic, even religious outcry. But to Uganda's great credit, AIDS sufferers there were seen simply as sick people in need of help. During times of terror, fighting men had carried AIDS around the country. Now, paradoxically, it was peace that helped it to spread. As the new regime took over in Kampala, travelling felt safe and people began to relax. Young people began to enjoy social life and 'night parties', with the inevitable drinking and promiscuity.

But away from Kampala the remains of Amin's mercenary army, now unpaid and with no love for Uganda, were on the loose. David had to walk home from Mbale one night when they were on the rampage and all road traffic had been halted. As well as looting, they were harassing any suspected Amin opponents. The Wakumire home became a place of refuge for many travellers escaping this rabble.

In the villages, people took merciless revenge on any soldier who came their way. Even in this peaceful rural landscape the smell of danger was everywhere. David's mother, Esther, lived alone, and when one of her neighbours was killed David begged her to move in with them. She refused. Esther had a cow, and she loved that cow too much to leave her. During the hours of darkness she was fairly safe in the house, but at dawn she would sneak out and hide amongst the bananas with her beloved cow.

David's stepbrother Samuel was driving the Bishop of Mbale and the bursar of Nabumali High School from Kampala to Mbale one day, but only got as far as Jinja. There Amin's men dragged them out of the car and pushed them into a crowded room in the barracks. From there men were being taken out one by one and killed. The bursar was first, followed by the Bishop. Then a soldier opened the door and hissed to those still inside, 'Run, all of you, they're coming to kill you.' They all ran – except Samuel. He didn't trust anyone, and hid behind the door.

By now it was dark. Samuel sneaked out of the empty room and found his way out of the building. He ran, throwing off his white shirt and trousers on the way. There was a shout: someone had spotted him. He crawled under a chain link fence, then carried on running. He hid all that night, naked, torn and hungry. The next morning he managed to alert a sympathetic stranger, begged a piece of cloth to cover his nakedness, and got a lift home. The bursar was given a proper burial, but the bishop's body was never found. Samuel never heard what happened to those who ran away.

As Edith learned more about women's struggles, now exacerbated by war, she became increasingly sympathetic, angry – and frustrated. There must be something she could do, but what? She felt so helpless. Her sister Christine's experience in 1985 unknowingly pointed the way forward.

Christine had been working as Secretary in the Mbale Mayor's office since 1976. She had always been a nominal Christian, but when she met Christ in person for the first time and acknowledged him as her Saviour, her first prayer was, 'God, I want to know something that I may be able to help others.' Five years she was given the opportunity.

From 1969, the Haggai Institute in Singapore has held a one-month course every year to train Christian women for leadership. Dr John Edmond Haggai of Atlanta, USA, recruited Christian faculty members and speakers for the course. Each sponsored participant could recommend someone for the following year. When Christine heard about this in 1985 she knew it was the answer to her prayers and sent in her application form. Two weeks later the answer came: she was too late. She wrote twice more, each time stressing that she was prepared to leave at a minute's notice. There was still no response. Christine's fourth letter simply asked that she be included in the next intake. In 1986 she was offered a place, with exactly two weeks to get ready. The next hurdle was the $250 fee. At that time in Uganda foreign currency was only available for VIPs, but Christine prayed about this, and got on with her packing. She never did discover who sent her the money from Rwanda, but says she'll know when she gets to heaven. She left with $700 in her wallet.

She went to Singapore to learn, but the first hard lesson was at Bombay airport. An Immigration Officer turned the pages of her passport, then looked up at her.

'I can't see your visa.'

Christine asked, 'Visa? What visa?'

'You can't enter Thailand without a visa.'

'But I'm not going to Thailand. I'm going to Singapore.'

'You're changing planes at Bangkok. And for that you need a visa for Thailand.'

'Well nobody told me that. What can I do?'

He shrugged. 'Get on the next flight home, I suppose.'

Handing the passport back to her, he waved her away. The grumbles of impatience from the long queue behind her changed to murmurs of sympathy.

For twelve hours Christine was trapped. She couldn't even contact Ethiopian Airlines, her carrier. A desperate phone call to the Haggai Institute in Singapore did the trick. Somehow they got the airline to sort things out. A day behind schedule, Christine arrived in Singapore.

At first she felt out of her depth amongst the hundred young and middle aged women at the Institute. She'd been educated to School Certificate level, but here she was mixing with teachers, doctors, lecturers, lawyers and pastors from all over the world. But God had chosen her to reach this place, and she was determined to make the best possible use of it. Every day was packed with lecturers, discussions and worship. She was astonished to see many of the women skip lectures, using their month in Singapore for a sightseeing and shopping spree.

On her way home Christine spent one night in Bombay. From the comfortable viewpoint of a good international hotel she was appalled to see people snatching leftover food out of the rubbish bins, and living on the roadside in cardboard boxes.

Christine's heart went out particularly to single women. From Singapore she learned to maximise her own skills, and to teach others to stand up, speak up and be useful. Her personal motto: 'Don't waste time on a pity party.'

1986 was a big year for David, too. In April AEE sent him to Zimbabwe for Reinhard Bonke's 'Christ for the Nations' conference. Every country in Africa was represented amongst the thousands in the big tent in Harare. Reinhard Bonke challenged them, 'This continent needs to experience the living Christ with miracles to challenge witchcraft and demonic forces.'

David lost a very good friend that year. The Revd John Wilson, AEE's Assistant Team Leader for Eastern Africa, had brought teams from Australia, Germany, USA and Great Britain to minister to the people of East Africa in a holistic way, sharing the word and feeding the masses in schools and rural areas. Before seeking ordination, John had been a successful businessman in the oil industry. In 1977 through AEE, he and his wife had worked for the 'Rehabilitation, Education and Training for Ugandan Refugees Now' (RETURN). Early in 1986 he and David worked together at a week-long workshop David had co-ordinated for church leaders in Kampala. On Saturday morning the friends said goodbye, and David left for Mbale. On Sunday he switched on the BBC news to hear that John had been shot dead at a road-block in Kampala. This was doubly shocking since a new government had been elected only a week before, and a time of peace had been expected. (A memorial seat in Coventry Cathedral's International Centre for Reconciliation recognises John's efforts for his country.) A few Amin supporters and other opposition factions were still at large, and gunfire could still be heard after dark in Kampala in early 1987.

When Colonel Gaddafi made a state visit to Uganda in September 1986, he led prayers in the Old Kampala Mosque, urging all Muslims to support President Yoweri Museveni.

The civil war had ended, but the fight against AIDS intensified. The President appealed to all sections of the community, including the churches, to help in the fight against this killer disease. In 1986 he toured the country to educate communities on the avoidance of the disease. AIDS prevention became a patriotic duty. The Ministries of Health, Education, Agriculture and Information formed the Uganda AIDS Commission in 1987. This was attached to the Prime Minister's office, but in the Mbale district always chaired by someone from a religious body.

Edith never found out who put her name forward for the Haggai Institute course in 1987. The application form asked, 'If you come for this training, what will you do with it?' Edith's answer: 'I will use it to build the capacity of Christian women teachers to give spiritual and moral teaching to children, as well as their subjects.'

David found the $250 Edith needed for the course by working and saving, and with a little help from friends. Edith realised later how perfect the Lord's timing had been. Shortly before she left in June 1987, she had been shaken by a nasty family incident. She and David had sold cows to buy timber for their new house. One of David's distant relatives claimed that David owed him money for the cows. Instead of discussing the dispute sensibly he commandeered the newly-purchased timber. In Singapore Edith faced the fact that she hated this man, and bitterness was hindering her relationship with God. She talked about this with Grace Sathyaraj, the Indian lecturer, who told her, 'If you hold bitterness against anyone in your heart, you'll never get close to God.' They prayed together. Edith needed to fast and pray to release this man and his family. She asked God to provide for their home some other way. This was to be a major turning point in Edith's life.

Both sisters were humbled to hear stories from women from other countries and cultures, some poorer than Uganda, their women leading an even harder life. In India, for instance, a wife is her mother-in-law's virtual slave, never allowed out of the house. It's not unknown for a mother-in-law to murder her daughter-in-law so that she can acquire a second dowry. Many unwanted girl children were killed at birth. In Arab countries, even in Christian circles, a wife must always walk behind her husband.

Grace told them: 'Women from the third world, God can use you in your own land to change the situation of your own people because you know the culture, the language and the issues affecting you. People from the developed world may have dollars and other resources, but these cannot be effective without you at the grassroots. So go back and use the skills you get here to make a difference in your community. You are being empowered to lift the status of women.'

Dr Haggai himself challenged them by satellite from Atlanta: 'As Christians, you should dream big with the Lord. He will make those dreams come true. As leaders, set goals that will influence other people to follow you, and if you have set goals that fit in with God's will, you'll find the right direction. In your leadership role, Jesus is the Way, the Truth and the Life. In Jesus we find God's will, and when we follow him he already knows the way, so what you're doing through Jesus is the truth. It may be difficult. The world may say it's impossible, illogical, irrelevant, but what Jesus says is the truth. He came to lift the oppressed, the marginalised and the poor to regain the status they are meant to have. As leaders you are going to influence others to go the right way and do the right things.'

Despite her serious intent, Edith couldn't help thinking about her family back home. She saw Singapore's thriving markets, compared them with Uganda's barren shops, and allowed herself two brief shopping trips. Her daughters were thrilled when they unwrapped their presents: three pairs of knickers each.

On their way home, Edith and her colleagues reached Addis Ababa only to discover that the airline had forgotten to make their onward booking. The Immigration Officer shrugged: they would just have to hang around for two days.

Now Edith had spent a whole month learning how to set goals and achieve them. Using her newly-honed skills, she demanded help from the Ugandan Embassy. Very soon the group were taxied to the Hilton Hotel, given comfortable rooms, fed, and promised seats on the next flight home. She had already learned a lesson that would stand her in good stead for the rest of her life: know your rights, be polite but firm – and persevere.

Edith's concern now embraced all the women of Uganda. She still needed to discover how God wanted her to use her new leadership skills, and David would be a part of that discovery.

David himself had had another adventure that year. At the end of a mission rally in Lilongwe, Malawi, he was asked to give a lady a lift home. Of course he agreed. He didn't know that she was a notorious prostitute who'd been tricked into attending the rally. Confused and ashamed, she admitted to David as they drove along that she had only half understood what she had heard, and been disturbed by it. Gently David explained the gospel to her, and before the car reached her home she'd committed her life to the Lord.

Once the excitement of her homecoming had subsided, David took Edith to the shores of Lake Victoria, where they sat on the beach and talked things over. She told David about the challenge thrown down to the women at Singapore on their last day by Mr Samuel George: 'People have spent money to get you here. How are you going to repay? You have to do something.' David replied, 'That sounds good: so do something.' They prayed together for wisdom and the Lord spoke clearly to them both: Edith must start a special ministry for women.

Widows who had been infected with HIV/AIDS were at the top of the needs list. Edith had always been aware of the degrading traditions of widowhood. Now she began to recognise their physical impact. The fight must start before women reached that point.

But first there were matters at home that needed attention. Their family was still growing. And there were many urgent calls for Edith's help outside the home – and Mbale.

African Recovery 1998

CHAPTER 14

1987-9 ~ refugees, foundation of UWCM

While Edith was at Nyondo, college tutors were being invited to qualify as trainers in AIDS awareness. As Tutor and teacher of General Science, Home Economics and Religious Education, Edith was an obvious choice. After a two-month training course on HIV/AIDS she became a National Facilitator. Selecting teachers from secondary schools and colleges, she trained sixteen teams of community volunteers to educate teachers and health workers. Her work involved flying to remote and dangerous regions – Soroti, Kapchora, Moroto and Namalu – with Mission Aviation Fellowship. In 1988 she spoke to soldiers in Soroti, pointing out something that few of them were aware of – that women were at much higher risk of HIV infection than men, for several reasons:

- A woman's traditionally subordinate role, limiting her right to refuse or control sexual activity (e.g. the use of a condom).
- A man's traditional 'entitlement' to multiple sexual partners within and outside marriage.
- The common defilement of young girls, whose membranes are fragile and apt to tear.
- Seminal fluid stays for a long time in the vaginal canal, giving prolonged opportunity for infection.

Teaching on AIDS became mandatory in primary schools, and Edith was responsible for 456 schools in the Mbale district. Drama was put to good use, Edith herself playing the part of the AIDS virus. Wearing a scary mask with threatening teeth, black gloves with long talons and an ominous tail dangling from her black costume, she had her young audiences screaming with horror – and delight. In some villages she followed up her teaching by showing the *Jesus* film. For many it was the first film they had ever seen. Edith still taught her normal subjects. It became a joke that if someone was looking for her in college and asked, 'Where's Mrs Wakumire?' they would be told, 'She's gone for AIDS.'

Edith witnessed the devastation caused by AIDS, even without sexual contact. Women and young girls who washed the open wounds of the sick were exposed to infection. Village medicine was rudimentary. Injections were given either with shared needles or by the traditional method – local medicine rubbed through a cut on the back of the hand. She recognised another dangerous tradition: decorating a woman's stomach with a tattooed 'string of beads', using a series of small razor cuts.

The Wakumires now cared for four foster children as well as their own four, and they could cope. But their home was thrown into turmoil as a result of rebel atrocities in the north. David's brother-in-law had married Margaret, a lady from the troubled northern region of Teso. They soon separated, but some of Margaret's relatives would occasionally visit the Wakumires. Edith had taught one of them, Robert, at Nyondo Teachers' College. News reached Mbale that insurgents had caught Robert and sliced off his ears, but he'd escaped south with his sister and his wife, Rose. Robert found safety and a teaching job in the Mbale region and Rose named her first daughter after Edith.

One of Edith's friends, Edith Obuda, married a Teso man, Epaphras. Edith Obuda was pregnant – and dying of cancer. Her baby boy was delivered by caesarean section shortly before she died. Epaphras joined the rebels in the North and was killed. Edith Obuda's parents took care of their orphaned grandchildren, including the new infant. In 1987 they fled from the rebels, heading for the Wakumire home. After a week of walking by day and sleeping in the bush by night, they were caught by the insurgents, who shot and killed the old man and his eldest grandson. Beaten almost to death and with a broken arm, Mrs Obuda managed to rescue the younger children. The rebels tracked them down, marched them back to the house, stripped it, carried off the chickens and goats, then put the survivors back in the house. Somehow Mrs Obuda escaped with the children and got a lift to Soroti, north of Mbale.

When David and Edith heard what had happened in the north they sent for Mrs Obuda and her grandchildren. They were expecting four, but the old lady arrived with an assortment of sons, grandchildren, her daughter and a sister's grandchild – nine in all. They had no choice but to squeeze them all into their three-roomed house. By now Stephen was at university, but Rose, another family orphan, had joined them. David and Edith slept in one room, their children in another, the nine visitors in the third – for three years.

Through David's work with AEE he was occasionally given some basics such as oil and flour. The neighbours became jealous and suspicious, reporting to the local government that the Wakumires were hiding rebels, but nothing came of this. The neighbours saw them as foreigners and treated the children spitefully.

Feeding nineteen people was a struggle. But the land was very fertile; cassava and beans were always available. They would cut the cassava into very small pieces and serve it on plastic plates. David and Edith would praise God and thank him before they tucked into those meagre helpings. They never lost their faith in a merciful Saviour.

There was a bigger problem than food; Mrs Obuda still played the part of matriarch, taking it for granted that she and her children were honoured guests who shouldn't be expected to help in the house or garden. She wouldn't allow David or Edith to discipline her children. Occasionally she would visit relatives and bring back a few peanuts, roasting these to share among her own children. But the Wakumire children, tantalised by the smell, never got a taste.

One refugee who remembers the Wakumires with gratitude is Sarah Inero. She was the same age as Solomon, about eleven at the time. Sarah remembers: 'We were included in every family outing. Uncle David and Mama Edith gave us presents and new clothes every Christmas, just like their own children.'

Sarah's formal schooling had been brief and interrupted, but David and Edith topped up her school fees until she'd finished O levels in Mbale, then went to a Kampala boarding school for A levels.

Two of Sarah's brothers had witnessed their father's murder. The older brother, Ezekiel, was the brainy one, but he never got over his bitterness. He refused David's offers of help, and was offended when he and the other refugee boys were asked to give a hand. He used to cry out to Edith, 'Why does God let me suffer like this? I don't want to be a refugee!' He did well in exams, and a well-wisher sponsored him for university. After dropping out for one year because of stress, he carried on and got a degree in Civil Engineering. Twenty years later Sarah says he still suffers from depression.

Sarah learned three important things from David and Edith: the first was determination. Her mother should have received a widow's pension, but because all their family papers had been destroyed she couldn't claim her entitlement. Sarah scoured government offices and found the deeds entitling her mother to land. At last she had a chance to grow food and make a modest income.

Secondly, Sarah learnt to be self-reliant. She worked hard and stayed single, determined to wait for the right Christian husband.

The third important thing Sarah learned was the love of music. Every day she looked forward to the time when Uncle David would bring out his guitar, and they would all join in their favourite hymns. Later Sarah wrote her own songs and earned a little money singing at private functions. She invested in a recording of her music, which soon paid for itself and started to make a profit.

David flew to Amsterdam in October that year for a meeting of Open Doors. When David reported on his work crossing the Uganda/Kenya border, Brother Andrew commended him, 'Brother David, you were brave to cross with those bibles to Uganda when circumstances were tough under Amin!'

When David and Edith built their present house along the Mbale/Tororo road in Wabukhasa village in 1989, it was built to last, a spacious, solid house of brick with a metal roof. They also built a grass-roofed home for the refugees nearby. Their visitors had enjoyed three comparatively easy years and didn't want to move, but they had no choice. David and Edith had helped one of the sons to get to university in England, another joined Youth With a Mission (YWAM). Two years later Mrs Obuda and her family moved back to their homeland in the north.

One night in their new home, the Wakumires were awakened by the crash of breaking windows, rattling doors, and aggressive voices demanding money. The family hid in the bathroom. Although the lock was broken, the attackers couldn't open the door, and gave up after four hours. David very quickly had the glass windows in the corridor blocked, and other windows fortified with wooden shutters.

Edith could have been forgiven for pushing her ambitions to one side, but the more she learned about the problems faced by women, the more determined she became. God hadn't brought her this far simply to sort out family problems. She had been trained for leadership. One third of all married women were in polygamous relationships, often pregnant against their wishes. A quarter of women in rural areas have never been to school. The church and MU seemed the right place to start. But MU didn't cater for the many battered women who were not formally married. Edith's focus was on human rights for all women, particularly those linked with HIV/AIDS. Some kind of organisation was needed. She resigned from the teacher training college where she'd been Tutor for ten years, confident that she had done her duty there.

With David's help Edith made a start. Together they decided on the name: Uganda Women Concern Ministry (UWCM). And the vision: to uplift the status of women. They wrote down the objectives:

- To provide educational and training opportunities for women and girls.
- To establish an effective grassroots counselling system, visiting, counselling and supporting women in families affected by AIDS.
- To sensitise and mobilise women to engage in income-generating activities that would improve their financial status and give them personal dignity.
- To support the basic needs of orphaned children and provide school fees for their education.

This was clearly going to be Edith's big life project. In September she brought sixty women together to discuss issues affecting every category of women – singles, widows, married and juvenile. Edith told them, 'Poverty isn't always the greatest problem; apathy is. We need to empower women through education and skills development so that they can make informed decisions. If you sit and wait to be given, you should know the consequences.'*

David planted the first seeds by giving five boxes of donated canvas shoes to be sold. This money covered the legal cost of registering the ministry, work that had already started in their garage. Every morning, after David had driven his car out of the garage, Edith would move a table and chairs in and start on the paper work. Even in the first few days people would walk for miles to ask for help. Those waiting outside early in the morning would be given breakfast in the house. This went on for about six months. That tiny garage was obviously inadequate. At first Edith used her own resources, then friends helped by visiting the sick and fetching water.

Next UWCM needed a governing body. David appointed himself Trustee and Advisor, but the rest of the board were all women. Grace Bwayo, a MU worker, was the first Chairperson. Grace Hamala, who worked with David as Children's Welfare Officer, was Treasurer. Others were Joy Wamboga, an English teacher at High School, and Phoebe Wanyama, who'd been to Singapore with Edith. (Later Phoebe was ordained and became Chaplain at Kyambogo University, Kampala.) Edith's sister Christine was also a board member. Stephen Nangosya, a social worker with experience of community development, was invited to draft a constitution. The rural area they planned to serve was too vast to cover on foot, so they employed Andrew, a retired taxi driver and a Christian, as their driver. Jessica, David's widowed sister-in-law, worked voluntarily in the office.

Edith was very clear: UWCM must serve the Lord at all times. And they must teach women to love their husbands. But she had a particular concern for single women. These are the strategies she'd learned in Singapore:

- Every opportunity should be taken to help others in need.
- They must be available whenever someone was sick and needed help with their children.
- They must use burials as an opportunity to tell people that the Lord has done great things.

- By providing medical outreach through the church many would be saved, and then it would be the Pastor's job to follow through.
- They must support families affected by AIDS, the leprosy of the day.

Work started long before the paperwork was completed. Edith wrote to a friend, 'With the two people who had first caught the vision we would go to visit a family, just fetch water for them, maybe boil water with tea leaves for them to drink, and through that we have had an opportunity to share a message with those people. And gradually many of the women came to know the Lord, and many who were contemplating suicide became saved and changed their attitudes and have lived for a long time. A child once asked, "Can you eat an elephant?" The answer is, "Yes, if I eat a little bit at a time, I can eat an elephant." In the same way, together we can preach the gospel. Through practice and through words we can call people to the Lord. We can make people's lives different and better.'

The Wakumire children were all in boarding school by 1989, and the refugees left in 1991. Perhaps now their home would be quiet and empty. Then Esaza arrived, but her story needs a chapter of its own.

*The Monitor, Sept 1998

CHAPTER 15

1982-2007 ~ Esaza's story

'I was three years old in 1982, and fierce fighting was going on around our home. I didn't know that we lived in what would be called the Luwero triangle, a place of horror. One day my mother and father went out to look for food. Soldiers stopped them and beat them up. Then they grabbed me and my brother. They hurt him, and he died. I don't know why they didn't kill me or why they kept me. As the army moved around they took me from camp to camp. One soldier would feed me for a while, then hand me on to another. I was soon big enough to fetch water and mix food, so I was put to work. And as I grew older, I could do more.

But when I was ten the civil war was over and the army disbanded. Nobody had any use for me any more, so they just dumped me. We were near Jinja, and they just left me at somebody's house. Nobody wanted me. The soldiers didn't want me, and neither did those people. Maybe they were afraid the soldiers would come back, so they couldn't send me away. They showed me a place I could sleep around the corner on their verandah. They even threw me a bit of old blanket. For food I would get a few leftover scraps, or I could forage for myself. I was always hungry. And then they used me for the heavy jobs, like collecting firewood and fetching water. That was the hardest of all. I had to take a big plastic jerrycan down to the River Nile and fill it, then carry it home on my head. It was very heavy. Sometimes they would beat me, but I never knew what I was supposed to have done wrong. Just for nothing, I suppose.

One day they sent me to get water as usual. There had been a lot of rain and the current was strong. The jerrycan was half full when suddenly I slipped, and the surge of water carried it away. I watched the jerrycan bob away from the riverbank. I ran as fast as I could, but the wide, swollen river soon carried it out of sight.

I was soaked, and sobbing with fear. I knew there'd be trouble when I got back to the house. When I did they shouted, "Where's the water?" I told them what had happened. "You mean you lost the jerrycan?" They beat me, then they said, "Go and find that jerrycan and don't come back without it. If you do, we'll kill you."

For hours I searched the river bank. Maybe the jerrycan had been caught in some reeds. But I couldn't find it. So how could I go back? And if I couldn't go back, where could I go? All I could do now was kill myself. I stepped into the river and kept on walking. The water was up to my ears. A few minutes more and I would not have been able to breath. Then I heard a voice, a girl's voice, shouting, "Hang on, I'm coming to get you out." I didn't move. This girl plunged into the river and pulled me to the bank.

She sat with me on the river bank and put her arm around my shoulders. I couldn't stop crying. I told her my life wasn't worth living any more. I told her about the beatings. She pulled me to my feet. "You come home with me," she said. "We'll look after you."

Her name was Irene. Her father and mother took me in, dried me, got me some fresh clothes and fed me. Irene was the one who told me that God loves all lost children. She told me about Jesus, and how he gave his life for me. I became a Christian.'

The story continues:
Irene's father was Patrick, brother of Andrew, the UWCM driver. When David and Edith heard Esaza's story, they were moved by compassion for the poor helpless ten-year-old. They asked their own four children how they would feel about having Esaza as a sister. Tamar was delighted. Only when they all agreed did they ask Esaza to be their daughter. Esaza settled happily into her new home, and they did what they could to make up for her complete lack of schooling.

Seven years later, while building a house in Mbale, Stephen Watiti employed some local boys as labourers. One of them from the Luwero district noticed Esaza, now seventeen years old, and saw a family resemblance. He had heard about the abduction fourteen years earlier, and suspected that her parents might still be alive. The boy went back to his village, found Esaza's family and told them that he thought he'd seen their daughter.

An old lady turned up at the Wakumire home and said she was Esaza's grandmother; she had come to take her home. But neither Esaza nor the Wakumire family trusted her. They told her they would speak to nobody but the girl's parents, and sent her away. Six months later an old man arrived, saying he was Esaza's father. With him was a lady with letters from local leaders explaining that the man had lost two children during the war. Somehow the facts didn't match the story. They told the man he must come back with the girl's mother. He returned with a very young lady called Florence, who was obviously not his wife. Annoyed and suspicious, David and Edith wouldn't allow them to see Esaza. However there was no denying the strong resemblance between Esaza and the young woman.

The following day the truth emerged – Florence was Esaza's aunt: it was Florence's older sister who had lost the two children. Again David and Edith insisted they must bring the mother. David gave them money to go back to their village, and two weeks later they returned with Florence's older sister. Now there was no doubt: the old man really was Esaza's father, and this woman her mother. The couple wanted to take her home immediately, but Esaza clung to David and Edith, refusing to leave. All that night she wept. After all she had suffered, she wanted to stay where she knew she was loved. When the parents insisted, Esaza threatened to kill herself. David calmed everyone down; Esaza must be allowed time to understand what had happened. He promised that when she was ready they would take her to them during the school holidays. Esaza had a few months to accustom herself to the fact that she had a biological family who had lost her and her brother, through no fault of their own. When the holidays came around, David and Edith hired a vehicle, and the whole family drove Esaza to Luwero.

Esaza's welcome at her parents' village threw her into a panic. She hadn't realised that her mother was related to the royal family of Buganda. For five days the whole village had been camped around the family home, feasting, drumming and dancing. She was greeted not simply as a lost child, but as royalty. The poor girl's emotions were in turmoil. When the moment came for her to decide – to stay or not to stay – David said the choice was hers. She wept, pleading to be taken home. David suggested they take her home until she was confident about such an enormous change. Her parents suggested a compromise: why not leave Tamar as well? That idea didn't go down at all well. They left, taking Esaza with them.

A year later she agreed to see her people again, but not alone, so Irene went with her for two weeks in the school holidays. They visited again the following year.

Esaza never saw her biological parents again. For her, Mama Edith and Uncle David are still Mum and Dad. They call her 'our miracle daughter'. She never made up for the years of schooling she'd lost, so they paid for her to do a tailoring course. Esaza didn't like the work, became restless, and went to live with an aunt in Kampala for a while. When she returned David and Edith found her a place to practise hairdressing, but she got into a relationship with a man from their village who promised to set her up in business in Kampala. He would go to Kampala every weekend to stay with her, but little came of his promises.

David and Edith had to accept that at eighteen she was old enough to make her own decisions. So they were shocked when someone rushed to their house one day to tell them that Esaza had come back to Mbale to bury her husband.

David hurried to the funeral, and nearly went mad when he heard his beloved girl referred to as 'the widow'. He became ill with grief. After the funeral Esaza disappeared once more. In 2007 Edith tracked her down in Kampala, and there was much rejoicing; their 'miracle child' had married a good man, and to add to their joy, Edith's visit coincided with the first birthday of Esaza's dear little son, Lennon. Once again there was much to thank God for, which David and Edith did with all their family. Esaza is determined that as Lennon grows up, he must be told her story, and made to understand how good can come out of evil, if one trusts the Lord.

CHAPTER 16

1990-91 ~ Edith's work expands

Uganda was regaining economic prosperity, but very slowly. The new government asked the Asians who had been expelled by Amin to return, promising them a safe welcome. Many were reluctant, but those who did return were treated honourably, with all confiscated property returned to them or their descendants.

The government of Uganda had from the beginning been very positive in its approach to AIDS, and in 1990 The AIDS Information Centre was opened in Kampala. The same year the AIDS Support Organisation (TASO) was founded by Noreen Kaleba, whose husband had died of AIDS; she knew how badly people in her position needed support. Noreen still carries on her work internationally from her home in Geneva.

Edith went for training with TASO, and helped to set up a branch in Mbale. Relations between TASO and UWCM were initially strained. The churches had been happy to support Edith's work through UWCM, but now she was working with this new secular organisation. Gradually each body found its niche. TASO would concentrate on the person who was HIV+ while Edith supported the whole family, including paying school fees. This good relationship had two big advantages. First, UWCM's Christian perspective enabled Edith to gain Tearfund's support. Secondly, when Edith headed the Diocesan Health Programme in 1989/90, she could refer pastors to TASO, who already had facilities.

Today women with AIDS, trained by UWCM, are working with TASO. They often use bible-based drama, using the stories of Sarah, Mary and Martha. All hints of rivalry died away.

Edith's week was now divided: two days with UWCM, two days with TASO, two days with Mbale Diocese.

In January 1991 President Museveni, the Minister of Health and other officials were invited to a Natural Resources Management project in Kampala, convened by the House of Bishops for church leaders. Edith was one of the delegates.

Challenging the clergy and bishops, the President said that AIDS was affecting everyone, including church members, and the first person a sick person turned to was his Pastor. Sometimes the Pastor himself had AIDS. The churches must give both teaching and practical help. He stirred up the Anglicans in particular, instigating a week of education. Teaching on AIDS in the churches became mandatory. Edith began to visit a different church each Sunday, talking about AIDS instead of the sermon. The Bishop asked her to spend three days every week co-ordinating health education in the Diocese, sensitising the church and the general population on HIV/AIDS.

While Edith was away the Wakumire home was attacked again. Two European visitors were in the house – and everyone knew that Europeans had money. At midnight thieves came and shouted through the windows, 'We're here! Open up!'

David peered through the window to see a gun pointed at him. He protested, 'We've got no money!' and threw a few coins out of the window, hoping this would satisfy them. But as he moved down the corridor they shadowed him, calling first through the sitting room, then the bathroom windows. By now the whole house was in an uproar, the children shouting and beating drums. The thieves tried to smash first the front door then the back, but by some miracle both locks held. One of the Europeans threw a glass of water at them through a broken window. They backed off, still shouting, 'These *wazungu* have money!' The attack went on for five hours. Neighbours ran to a nearby village and alerted a soldier. He ran back with them and fired into the air. The thieves escaped, throwing away their guns as they ran. Toy guns. The next day David had strong metal doors and shutters fitted to the house.

European visitors brought another problem – for Stephen Watiti.

Stephen had always been a modest, helpful young man. Visitors would see him working quietly in the garden or sweeping the compound, assume he was the houseboy, and dump a pile of dirty clothes for him to wash – politely, of course! For a young man with only one shirt, this seemed a bit hard, but Stephen didn't mind. What he did mind was being taken for granted. And Edith sided with him when he objected to washing two items – the women's intimate underwear, and men's smelly socks. So Edith laid down three rules: firstly, Stephen would do visitors' laundry, except for those two items. Secondly, there was to be no smoking in the house, and thirdly, visiting uncles mustn't bring young ladies into the house.

By now one and a half million people in Uganda were HIV+ (positive), eighty percent of them between the ages of fifteen and forty-five. UWCM was officially launched as a registered charity in 1991 with fifteen local women. Their strategy was clear: first identify your community and talk to the church leaders about the need for practical help as well as preaching. They trained thirty church-based Christian volunteers called Community Counselling Helpers (CCH). Two days of rigorous training covered HIV/AIDS, First Aid and hygiene, nutrition, home care and children's needs, counselling, women's rights, the use of resources and income-generating activities. Each CCH was committed to spending two days every week on this work. UWCM staff would go to different churches and teach about those needs, using Matthew 25:32-46, in particular verse 40: *'Whatever you did for the least of one of these brothers of mine, you did for me.'* HIV/AIDS must no longer be seen as a curse, the result of an immoral life. The first male CCH to be trained was the Revd Samwiri Wabulakho, now Bishop of Mbale.

David and Edith built a grass-roofed office next to their home. They could have rented premises in the centre of Mbale, but Edith declined. She explained, 'Our target group are rural women. First they have the problem of getting to town, then they'd feel uncomfortable when they got there. So we'll stay close to them.'

For most of the women tested positive for HIV, lack of status was the biggest problem. These were angry women, and many wanted revenge. A young girl sent to work in Kenya came back with AIDS, only to be abused by her family. One night she chased her mother away, got her father drunk, and slept with him. The next time her parents had the nerve to abuse her she told them what she'd done, and what to expect. All three died of AIDS. One well-to-do family treated their housemaid badly, not knowing that she had AIDS. The girl drew blood from her own finger and injected it into their children. Again, she waited until they abused her again before hurling the truth at them. In a third case, a single mother shouted at her teenage daughter once too often. The girl got her revenge by sleeping with her mother's boyfriend, infecting both him and her mother with AIDS.

Many men with AIDS deliberately infected others out of sheer spite. A rich man would seduce first one schoolgirl and then another, infecting half the school before he died. This was their warped way of attacking healthy young men. Poverty and AIDS usually form a downward spiral. Suicide was the first option for many women. But Edith discovered an unexpected bonus: when a widow is helped to face the future, she very often finds more freedom in widowhood than she has ever known as a married woman.

The MU Secretary appeared in Edith's office one day. 'You must come. There's a lady who needs your help badly.' Together they rushed to Joyce's village. Her husband had died of AIDS, leaving her with six children, plus four children of her co-wives. His family had kicked her out, blaming her for passing on the disease to him. She had no legal right to any property left by him: if she died her children would be both homeless and penniless. Using what little cash and energy she had left, she had bought a large bottle of strong pesticide. Joyce was mixing this with orange juice when her youngest son came home from school. He recognised the smell, asked her what she was doing, but got no reply. Seeing the empty bottle he put two and two together and ran out screaming, 'Mummy wants to kill us! I don't want to die!' Ashamed, Joyce poured the poison away. In desperation she turned to the MU, who sent her to Edith. Joyce tells the rest of her story:

'But for UWCM, I would have been devastated with fear, poverty and hopelessness. With the money they gave me I followed their advice and hired a stall in Nakaloke market where I sell vegetables. I also bought cloth, thread and wool to make tablecloths. With the sales from these I get enough money to support our family needs.'

Next she planted eucalyptus trees and started brickmaking. She and her family survived, she became a Christian, and UWCM trained her as a CCH. She's still working – and smiling.

CHAPTER 17

1991-2 ~ Edith goes to Europe, UWCM grows

When Edith first visited Europe in May 1992, she was only there for the ride. David had gone to visit supporters of CCP and talk to Tearfund, and his sponsors had invited him to bring his wife.

Edith stepped off the plane at Heathrow on a chilly spring morning wearing a warm skirt and overcoat, but by the second day her legs were aching with cold. She turned to David in despair.

'My legs are frozen: please can I borrow a pair of your trousers?'

David pretended to be shocked.

'What? A woman, my wife, wear trousers? You know that's forbidden in our culture. Do you want me to report you to my mother?'

They laughed, but Edith was happy to break that particular taboo – and stay warm.

No sooner had they unpacked in Coventry than David fell ill. A doctor was rushed to the house, diagnosed malaria and prescribed the appropriate drugs, but four hours later David's tongue had swollen alarmingly. A hurried blood test revealed that David was diabetic, and only then were they able to sort out the right treatment. (Malaria plays havoc with the blood sugar levels.) He was soon able to carry on with his business in Coventry, then on to Holland for meetings with his Dutch sponsors. He and Edith found time to enjoy the flower auctions and cheese factories. David chuckled when a two-year-old Dutch girl patted his cheek, asking, 'Are you made of chocolate?'

Back in England, Edith met John Horton, Director of Tearfund's East and Southern Africa regions. When Edith told him the extent of her vision, John asked her to send a proposal. Tearfund were so impressed that they approved a donation of £30,000 from their Children's Emergency Fund, to be used at Edith's discretion. She shared this between salaries, office expenses and school fees, later extending help to families. A new vehicle was ordered from Japan and shipped to Uganda. Edith always thanked God – and Tearfund – for this early support when she was still learning the ropes of fundraising.

Edith's sister Freda was now working at the Uganda High Commission in London, so the two were able to enjoy some time together, including a boat trip on the Thames. Freda told her all about being invited to tea at Buckingham Palace, and shaking hands with the Queen, Prince Philip and Princess Diana. When they weren't with Freda, David and Edith stayed with Elizabeth Swarbrick in Lancashire.

David and Edith attended an AIDS Care Education and Training (ACET) conference in London. The link between cancer and HIV had been recognised by Dr Patrick Dixon, author of *Truth about AIDS* and founder of ACET. In Uganda he saw the churches struggling with very basic questions: had God sent AIDS as a punishment? Was it safe to touch people? Was it safe for communicants in church to drink from one cup? One Anglican priest, Revd Gideon Bymugisha, was the first to 'come out' in 1992 and announce that he was HIV+.*

Anthony Kasozi was still at school when his family escaped from Uganda during the Amin regime. He completed his education in the UK, married an English wife, then interrupted a successful business career to help establish ACET. In 1992 he left London with his wife and two-year-old daughter, set up a home in Kampala and opened a branch of ACET in Uganda. Anthony and a colleague travelled across the country, talking to Christians and encouraging them to discuss these issues amongst themselves. He knew that advice from an outsider, even a native Ugandan, wasn't helpful.

Back in Africa, Edith went to Nairobi for a three weeks' course for social development ministries and management skills. Edith had taken her overseas travels in her stride, but she still shudders when she remembers that nightmare journey to Nairobi. The rackety and overcrowded bus left Mbale after dark, hurtling through the night along cracked, unlit, potholed roads. There were frequent long stops, first at a roadblock on the Kenya border, where all passengers had to disembark for questioning, their papers and luggage searched, then long stops to buy food – bottles of soda, samosas, bananas, peanuts etc – and use the primitive toilet facilities. Edith arrived at 6 a.m., shaken and shivering in Nairobi's frosty high-altitude air, thankful that David had insisted she take the overcoat she'd been given in England.

On Anthony Kasozi's recommendation, ACET made a donation towards the cost of a hut for counselling near the Wakumire home, enough to pay for the foundations and brickwork. A friend gave a further £500, and Anthony encouraged them to seek help from other organisations.

Two of Edith's old friends, Pastor Patrick Gidudu and his wife, Hannah, were in the UK doing their Masters degrees. In England they met Joy Thomas and Doreen Morgan, volunteers with ACET. The two women told Patrick how eager they were to see what the churches and other bodies in Uganda were doing. Within minutes Patrick had picked up the phone, dialled Edith's number, and arranged a three-week visit. Their impact in Uganda was enormous. With a simple flannelgraph and pictures they taught the facts about HIV/AIDS, then how to use the word of God in a crisis. People who suspected they were HIV+ came for counselling, and many became Christians. For Edith this confirmed the need for a Christian approach. Only Christ gave the hope these suffering people needed. Joy visited again later with her husband, the Revd Ray Thomas.

Edith's work began to attract valuable young professionals. ACET had asked Edith to help with their research, and for this she employed Richard Wamembi, a young Christian with a degree in Social Work and Administration. When he finished that job, she kept him on and trained him in children's work.

Twenty-three-year-old Lornah Wamono became Children's Secretary, but also oversaw the goats project. Lornah, Edith and other staff members went to Jinja for a Christian counselling course run by the Australian Institute of Family Counselling.

Robert Mortimer of Oasis Trust reported after a visit, 'Edith's seven staff provide help for AIDS orphans and counselling to the families. In 1992 they used £30,000 from Christmas Cracker to buy a four wheel drive truck – vital when visiting the small homesteads in the Mbale region where they work.' He was asked to pray at one home he visited. 'It was one of those unforgettable moments when words seem inadequate. When we came into the open again we saw a line of graves: it is the custom in Uganda to bury the family within the homestead.'

When one of TASO's clients, his four wives and two children died of AIDS, his remaining wife stumbled into the UWCM office in distress. Merabou had been left with the remaining twenty children, including her own ten. Her five daughters were about to be 'inherited', i.e. snapped up as wives or concubines. UWCM renovated her house on behalf of the church and helped her to keep her girls at home. She and her children became Christians before she died in May 2000. By then most of them were in primary school, high school or college. UWCM supported the family until the older siblings could take care of the younger ones.

Something new and exciting happened in November 1992, when a hundred orphans and vulnerable children were brought together in Mbale for a few days of fun and good food. But more important was an opportunity to express their grief and come to terms with what had happened to them. They were shown love, and hope for the future. This was the very first Children's Conference.

With the funding received from Tearfund, UWCM were able to open a child sponsorship programme for a hundred children.

David had donated the land, Tearfund enabled them to put up a permanent office building, and the staff expanded to ten. In two years Edith's life had changed beyond recognition, for the good. But the shadow of AIDS was about to darken their own hopes and dreams.

*He was awarded the Niwano Peace Prize in 2009 (*Church of England Newspaper 15.05.09*)

Edith's family (Ch3) Back: Ezerena and Philip, Front: Freda, Margaret, Christine, Edith, Florence

David and Edith's wedding, 4 May 1974 (Ch10)

Tamar

Esther

Florence and Edith 2007

*Stephen and Naomi Watiti
2006 (Ch28)*

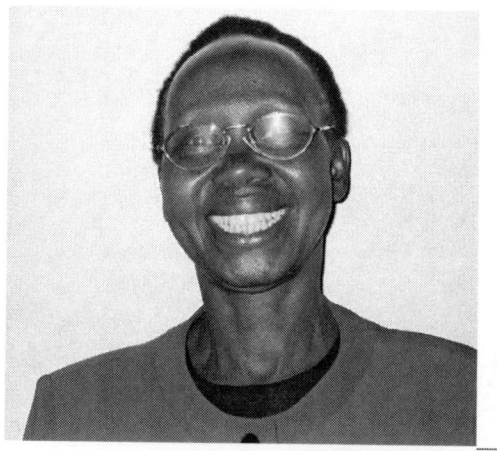

Edith's sister Christine

Nancy (Ch33)

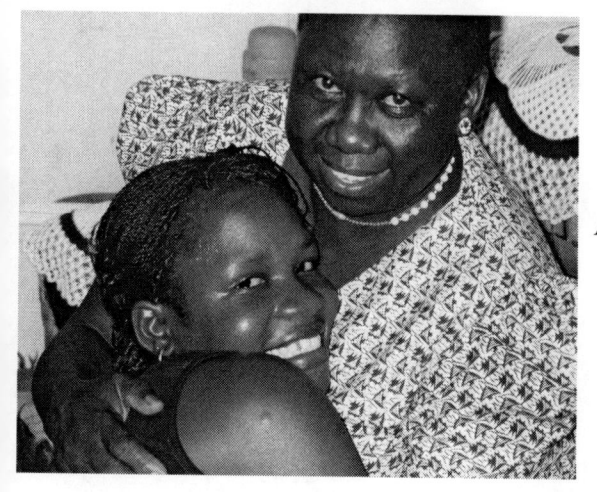

Edith and Esaza reunited (Chs15&33)

Sarah Watundu at Porridge & Prayer Club (Ch19)

A family (and house) in need of UWCM's help

Bishop Samwiri Wabulakho of Mbale – UWCM's first male volunteer

Jackson and family (Ch31)

Faith House

David with Edith at her graduation 2007

CHAPTER 18

1993 ~ AIDS in the family; Edith goes to Canada

Stephen Watiti had been David and Edith's pride and joy. When he became seriously ill and HIV+ in 1992 they were devastated. Stephen had contracted the disease while working as a doctor. His wife, Margaret, pregnant with their third child, was also unwell. Their seven-year-old son had already died of sickle cell disease and three-year-old Deborah was the only healthy member of the family. Edith visited them in April when she was in Kampala for an all-Africa consultation on AIDS and the Church. It broke her heart to see her beloved foster-son wasted and ill, and she did everything within her power to comfort him. But the following month she put family and UWCM problems to the back of her mind when she set off on another long overseas journey, this time alone.

Excited and expectant on three counts, she boarded a Canadian Air flight for Toronto. Firstly, she had been invited to an international conference on bereavement at Kings College, London, Ontario. Marks McAvity, an old friend and school teacher from Nabumali, had arranged further visits for her to exchange ideas on how HIV/AIDS was being handled. Secondly, she would spend six weeks travelling across Canada from the furthest points east to west, with many stops in-between. Thirdly, and by no means least, she would be meeting old friends.

The first of these friends were Gary and Ruth Ann Murray, who had been teachers at Nabumali High School twenty-five years earlier. At their home in Toronto Edith was plunged into two frantic days of visits and talks before leaving by train for London, Ontario.

At the Kings College conference, Edith was the only African among delegates from eleven countries. She gave a paper on 'A Ugandan Perspective on Death and Dying', emphasising the challenge of helping ageing parents whose children had died of AIDS, leaving them with orphaned grandchildren. She also gave a workshop on how she dealt with children whose parents were dying of AIDS.

Edith had a brief and thrilling respite on board the *Lady of the Lake* at Niagara Falls, screaming with excitement at the awe-inspiring height and expanse, the deafening boom of the thundering falls, enveloped by the misty spray – and rejoicing in God's wonderful creation.

Back in Toronto, eight visits were crammed into four days in this busy modern city. Edith inspected hospitals and community services covering every kind of AIDS help involving education, spiritual care, counselling and medical. Edith was moved by some of the personal stories she heard on these visits. One Pastor, thrown out of his church because he was homosexual, had founded a new church, a church that welcomed anyone, regardless of their sexual orientation.

She had looked forward to meeting the children with AIDS at the Children's Hospital, perhaps making them laugh and giving them a hug. So it was a shock to be told she couldn't even see them. It was even more distressing to learn that some parents chose not to visit; they didn't want anyone to know their children were there. For Edith the thought of those children being ill with no-one to hug or comfort them was almost unbearable.

At St John, Newfoundland, Edith talked to students and lecturers at the Hospital Science Centre. She was interviewed on radio, and the local newspaper told her story. At St Clare's Hospice and St John's Home Care Group she saw palliative care in action. She talked to the Newfoundland's AIDS Committee about fundraising. This most easterly corner of Canada was cold and foggy, but the city of St John was beautiful and the people warm and welcoming.

She was met in Halifax, Nova Scotia by her hosts, the Sisters of Charity, who took her first to a nearby beauty spot, Peggy's Cove. Edith was thankful for this break when she realised the enormous challenge she next had to face. At an AIDS Mastery weekend retreat for thirteen men and four women, all gay or lesbian, and with HIV/AIDS, Edith was the only 'straight' person, apart from two Facilitators. The theme was: 'positive living – one day at a time'. Not one of them was a Christian. Edith made it clear that she was there simply as an observer, a Christian eager to learn how best to support the angry and segregated. They respected that. Sitting on the floor around Edith, they would talk, and she would listen.

The only elderly person, bisexual, spoke about his responsibility for both his wife and his male partner. The younger men were frank about how they'd been sexually abused, usually by a father figure. They told Edith how after actually enjoying the experience they had turned against women, and could find comfort only with other men. Two had been thrown out when their parents discovered they were both HIV+ *and* homosexual. One told Edith, 'I never heard my mother say she loved me: I don't hear from her. This is the first time I've been close to a woman who would listen to me.' The four women – all on drugs, drinking, smoking and overweight – had been rejected by their families.

All this was a big culture shock for a woman of Edith's church background. Edith simply listened and loved and told them stories about Uganda. As the retreat ended Edith asked for permission to pray with them. Then each one asked Edith for a hug. Some said this was the first time they'd ever been enfolded in a woman's loving arms. They wrote her this farewell note: 'Although we are not Christians, we have loved you. You have been a mother to us.' What she learned there changed her attitude forever.

At Montreal Edith was driven from the airport to speak at three schools, then to the Montreal General Hospital to meet researchers and doctors who were about to depart for an AIDS conference in Berlin. Edith was interviewed on radio. Everywhere she went she shared her stories of the women and children of Uganda, and of Christ's love.

In Montreal her hosts at a convent gave her a farewell gift of money towards her expenses, their donation made up to $600 by a private individual.

Edith then flew across thousands of miles of Canada – over the lakes and Rocky Mountains – to reach Vancouver. There she was overjoyed to be met by more teachers from Nabumali – Margaret and Marks McAvity. Margaret had been Edith's teacher and Marks had taught David physics. At Christ Church Cathedral and two services in St Mary's church, Metchosin, Edith made good use of the ACET video 'Sharing the Challenge'. She had lunch at the Native Canadian Centre.

There was time to relax when Margaret and Marks took her by ferry to their home at Galiano on Victoria Island, where Margaret cooked Edith's favourite food – chicken in peanut sauce. Margaret introduced Edith to a woman doctor, Dr Sydney Sparling, wife of Dr Jim Sparling. Jim specialised in lung diseases, and spent some time each year at Mengo Hospital, Kampala. The next time Jim and Sydney were in Uganda they called on David and Edith.

Back in Uganda Edith soon found a good use for the $600 from the Sisters in Montreal. When the Ugandan army was downsized, each ex-soldier had been given, along with their demobilisation pay, iron sheets to help them build new homes. Many sold these for quick cash, and Edith acquired a hundred of them with the $600. They were used when it came to building the new UWCM office.

Dr David Evans, a specialist in HIV/AIDS, came to assess UWCM's work for Tearfund and saw for himself the desperate needs in the communities. Back in England he reported that UWCM were operating at an increasingly professional level, but with one old typewriter in a small, primitive office. Further help was agreed.

While Edith was on a training course in Biblical Counselling in Nairobi, their home was attacked for the third time. Late one night David heard dogs barking, and saw a policeman in the compound holding a gun. After this incident David asked for, and got, a police post in the neighbourhood. This was a huge relief to the villagers, who had been nervous for a long time. It was too easy for thieves to hide amongst the Eucalyptus trees, then leap out on passers-by. Perhaps now they would enjoy some peace.

Despite the seriousness of the situation, the family couldn't help chuckling about another family story. Edith's nephew ran a burglar-proofing business in Mbale, using his own house as a showcase. One dark night thieves cut round his burglar-proof door with metal saws and removed it. Isaac managed to escape, but realising that this was a poor advertisement for his business, he made some very hasty adjustments to the system.

In December, UWCM held their second Children's Conference

at Nabumali Boarding School. Again children enjoyed games, music, fun and bible study. There was also serious teaching about boy/girl relationships, hygiene and sex. But what six-year-old Dan Jabani remembered most was, 'I have never eaten such a good meal. Auntie, this is good.' After being given a blanket and a bar of soap, Simon remarked, 'We can now sleep comfortably and be able to wash and keep clean.'

For years Edith had prayed that she might learn to love Soferesi, and that her aunt would come to know the blessing of knowing Christ. Both prayers were answered in 1993. Edith realised that although they had been badly treated in Soferesi's care, the children themselves had shown little love. She and Christine talked about this, remembering the many spiteful, hurtful things they'd said and done.

It was Christine who broke through the emotional barrier and talked to Soferesi about God's love, just as she had done with Anzerena. She visited the old lady and apologised for all the things she'd done to make her aunt's miserable life even more miserable. At last the poor woman broke down and confessed the lack of love in her life, and how she now longed for it. Christine had the comfort of hearing Soferesi accept Jesus and his love, and was in the Mbale church when she was baptised that year.

On 7 January 1994 Stephen Watiti's wife and her new baby died of AIDS. Margaret's family showed nothing but hatred for Stephen: he had caused their daughter's death. David and Edith helped with Margaret's funeral, the usual expensive affair. His housekeeper stayed on to look after him and Deborah. It took years for Stephen to pick up the pieces of what seemed to be a ruined life, but they helped him through this time of anguish. They never stopped loving him, or trusting a loving Lord. Edith asserted, 'He's a doctor, he's a Christian, and he's our son.'

CHAPTER 19

1994 ~ the foundations of Faith House

David Wakumire once joked, 'I'm in a bigamous marriage: I'm married to both Edith AND the UWCM.' Edith's name may not appear in every story from now on, but she is the driving force behind every one.

The work was growing rapidly. In 1994 the United Nations Development Programme (UNDP) were looking for local groups combating HIV/AIDS and UWCM were one of twenty chosen. Edith attended their workshop in Naivasha, Kenya, for six days in March. UWCM's grant of £5,800 was one of the smallest. But it was enough to start a piggery. They started with two pigs, male and female, passed on two of the first litter of piglets, and so on. This scheme helped many families, and UWCM's pigs won first prize at the 1994 Mbale Agricultural Show. The UNDP were so impressed that they gave a further donation the following year, enough to pay for a breeding shed.

The words 'empowering women' are repeated time and time again in UWCM's promotional literature. They gave two Women's Associations money for trading produce, enabling them to earn a few shillings of their own for the first time in their lives, boosting their self-confidence and giving them some independence. But Edith cautioned, 'The way women tell others can be a deterrent, because we're dealing with a society that has been male-dominated for too long. It needs a gradual process and more awareness so that women can play a complementary rather than a competitive role with men. Arguing doesn't make people understand. Talking and listening does.'

But male attitudes weren't going to change overnight. That year the Constitutional Assembly of Uganda rejected an amendment providing that upon dissolution of a marriage, both the husband and wife should share equally any property acquired during the marriage. (This amendment wasn't passed until 2006.) For this reason whenever UWCM give a married woman a project, she is visited at home in her husband's presence. Both must understand why she's getting the project, and the benefits the whole family will receive.

The year brought huge changes in the lives of two Sarahs. The first Sarah tells her own story:

'My troubles began in 1991 when my co-wife fell ill and died. I was suspected of having bewitched and killed her. The intense hatred from relatives and neighbours almost crushed me. My immediate plans were to flee from home, but economic insecurity and the love for my children forced me to stay.

'My misery was aggravated by the death of my husband the following year. Our immediate family had not realised that AIDS had struck our home, and so they continued to vent their anger on me for having caused two adult deaths in a short period. I went to AIDS Information Centre, Mbale, and had my blood screened. I was found HIV+. You can imagine what I felt. Then the children… Oh, the children!

'A friend advised me to go to the CCP. They directed me to Mrs Edith Wakumire. The depth of love and concern with which Edith and her staff welcomed me melted away the burdens on my heart. I had not known I could ever find a place where I could be accepted or even understood. I was fed and comforted. UWCM staff regularly visit to counsel us, bring us material help and advise us on income-generating activities. With the help of my aged father-in-law and children I have raised poultry and grow food crops to keep my family going. UWCM have sponsored our seven children in schools and this gives me peace of mind – the children's future is secure if UWCM prospers. God be praised! I have learnt to live beyond this world and to see my coming death as a gateway to heaven.'

The second Sarah is Sarah Watundu, who turned to the UWCM in desperation when she fell ill in 1994. She had been HIV+ since 1989, and her husband had died leaving her with ten children. The four youngest were still at home. Bedridden, bad-tempered and trusting nobody, Sarah knew she was dying. She was only thirty-three. Edith visited her and set up a caring scheme. It was a wonderful 'Godincidence' that Esther Nilly, Edith's foster-daughter, with her gift of endless patience, became her chief carer. In Esther's life nothing is ever done without prayer. It took two weeks to persuade Sarah to have an AIDS test, and another two weeks of waiting to get Sarah to face reality and verbalise her fears.

When the dreaded answer did come, Sarah wept. She begged Esther not to tell anyone. Patiently, gently, Esther persuaded her to talk to her parents. They'd just buried another daughter and were understandably distraught. UWCM paid her medical bills and helped her to break the news to the children. Sarah had one big advantage: her CD4 count was high enough for her to benefit, first from Septrine and later from Antiretroviral (ARV) treatment, the side effects of which can be worse than the symptoms of the disease. (HIV damages cells in the immune system, including those called CD4 helper cells. The measurement of the count of these cells is used to monitor a person's immune status and check how advanced the disease has become.) While Sarah was still bedridden Esther, Edith and Lornah would clean and feed her, and as they cared, they taught.

Not only did Sarah survive – she blossomed. UWCM trained her as a CCH. She and her new friends searched the neighbouring villages and found eighteen people bedridden. These CCH were trained to clean homes and bodies (wearing gloves) twice a week. They made tea and porridge for the sick and taught families how to carry on. Counselling slowly overcame prejudice. Most of the eighteen died leaving orphans.

Her infectious smile soon made Sarah's home a magnet for all the village children. Each one was given a smile, a drink, a bite to eat, and above all, a listening ear. When the house filled to overflowing, Edith found her a bigger house on a bigger plot. Sarah was trained in First Aid and given a few non-prescriptive remedies. One big attraction was Aspirin, the answer to many everyday aches and pains.

Esther Nilly had a better idea: for hungry children, wouldn't a bowl of porridge do more good than Aspirin? The neighbours thought Esther was crazy. What was the point of porridge? But Sarah took the suggestion to heart. She started to provide porridge once a week for forty of her young visitors, and carried on for the next two years.

Maths had never been Edith's strong point. And she had more important things to do than sort out a finance system growing in complexity every day. It seemed like the Lord's provision when Agatha, who had a diploma in Accounts, joined UWCM and stayed for five years. Edith started to hold seminars on the value of making a will.

After another visit to Tearfund in 1994, Edith started planning new offices for UWCM, a single story office block with one large conference room, a wash room and seven or more small offices off a central corridor. Within six months the basic structure was up and roofed (using those iron sheets bought with the money from the Sisters in Montreal) and water and electricity installed. But it would take a little longer, and the help of more friends, to complete. The name of the new building was decided: Faith House.

New links were being formed through Tearfund. One branch in North Somerset collected used hand sewing machines, and Tearfund paid for their transport to Uganda. When they heard that Edith's counsellors could literally cover more ground if they had bicycles, they raised enough to pay for six.

In June Edith spoke at an ACET conferences in England and Scotland. When she spoke at Aberdeen, Joan Over was so moved by Jesska's story that she wrote out a cheque for £1,000 on the spot. Jesska herself wrote in a 1995 newsletter:

'At the death of my husband I was devastated. The responsibility I had ahead of me increased my grief. I had three sets of twins and three other children, and a number of relatives to support on a very small piece of land. I was compelled to dig for neighbours and also do odd jobs to feed my family. UWCM came to our rescue and bought us one-and-a-quarter acres of productive land. I can now grow enough food for my family. I have a stall in the market where I sell fish. School fees and medical care are catered for by UWCM. I hope to make bricks for the construction of our house.'

Joan's cheque paid for the land, seeds, and a house. There was money left over for three of Jesska's children to be trained in building skills. She and her family are still thriving.

The Matron of a hospice in England had a big problem. Some of her staff were alarmed at the prospect of anyone HIV+ being admitted to the hospice. She said, 'A lot of anger and ignorance were being thrown around. Spouses in particular had not wanted their wife/husband to be in contact. It was into this environment that Edith came, and by the end of the day people's attitudes had changed. She didn't challenge anyone, just spoke about her faith and her project. She showed the film "Accepting the Challenge" which had been made in Uganda for World AIDS Day, Edith's work being part of the video. One person in particular, who had considered AIDS to be the judgement of God, was very touched by it all, and made a contribution towards Edith's work.'

A newsletter dated May 1995 gives a clue to Edith's desperate needs for funds to pay for their many training events: sixty guardians met in May to discuss child support, thirty CCH completed their training, twelve teachers attended a weekend of Workshops for Youth which resulted in Anti-AIDS clubs in their schools, 160 children attended the third Children's Conference in November and on 22 December the Central Government Representative of Mbale District was Guest of Honour when thirty-nine clients got together.

Training events such as these required teaching materials, attendance allowances, transport and food, which all had to be paid for. Edith explained, 'UWCM provides good meals on such gatherings to make the clients happy and loved. One client said, "A person like me, without the help of UWCM, where would I get such a delicious meal?"'

The theme of the Children's Conference was: 'The fear of the Lord is the beginning of wisdom'. Each child was given a blanket to take home. The Local Council Chairman pledged his support, and gave six bags of cement towards the new building.

The Wakumire home suffered its fourth attack. After a fight about a girl, the culprit crashed through the fence into David and Edith's compound. They heard a shot, then silence. The following morning his body was on their verandah, guts spilling out, and a piece of torn trousers on the barbed wire. After that they planted a hedge of Cayaple, a shrub whose branches are twisted to make a tight, strong barrier. Finally they installed a lockable metal gate to keep the compound secure at night.

David and Edith broke with another strong tradition by having their boys circumcised medically instead of taking part in the traditional rite-of-passage, a ceremony now being advertised as a tourist attraction!

Held in January on alternate years, it involves the pagan sacrifice of a goat for each boy. One visitor watched dozens of young men between the ages of twelve and fourteen, their faces painted white, jogging along the road to Mbale for the ceremony, hundreds of supporters singing and drumming alongside them. The boys are given alcohol to lessen the pain, and afterwards wear skirts for comfort. The dancing and drumming goes on all night.

The Wakumires knew the insidious effects this tradition can have. Boys can be heard bragging, 'I'm a man now. I can do what I like. I don't have to go to school. Nobody can make me. And I can have sex if I like. Nobody can stop me.' Conversely, at the 2009 Children's Conference one boy challenged Paul Makheti, the Child Programme Officer: 'Once a boy is circumcised, some parents force him to marry and also stop him from eating food in their home. How do you help such children?'

There was another, more practical danger. Often a number of boys undergo the ritual at the same time, every cut performed with one knife, increasing the danger of spreading infection. In February 2007 Dr David Serwadda of Rakai Hospital, Uganda reported that trials conducted in South Africa, Kenya and Uganda showed that circumcision reduced HIV infection by 50-60%. He said, 'Circumcision should be promoted as an integral part of the Abstinence, Be Faithful, or Use a Condom (ABC) approach.'* David and Edith now teach these facts about circumcision. One of their aims is to help families finance the medical circumcision of their sons at a younger age.

One sign of hope was that Stephen Watiti, although still not well, was back at work.

*The Weekly Observer, Kampala, 22.02.07

CHAPTER 20

1995 ~ England, the churches and Solomon's eye

When Alan Dunningham of Tearfund saw what Edith had done about a new building and her fundraising efforts, he was very impressed. The car bought from the first budget had been damaged in an accident, and needed replacing. So Alan went home and dug deeper to find more funds for another vehicle.

A Tearfund team from the UK visited five of the projects they had supported. One team member, Terry Game, was thrilled to see some of the sewing machines sent by her church being used, as well as heaps of fabric, patterns, thread and other AIDS. Of all the projects they visited, UWCM affected Terry the most. She admired the practical, loving way they worked and the results they were achieving. Present at their weekly gathering for prayer and bible study, Terry felt the Holy Spirit at work. She was convinced that their unwavering Christian faith was the basis of their commitment.

Another member of that team was Bridget Withell, a nurse specialising in palliative care. She and Terry became friends, a friendship that is still bearing fruit for UWCM.

Some of the local churches were puzzled. They had understood that Edith's commitment was to teach about AIDS in the churches, but now she seemed to have endless funds to spend on school fees for all and sundry, a new office, a piggery and a vehicle. Surely this aid was meant for the church? Especially the vehicle: MU should have a share in that. And Edith was a volunteer with TASO. Was she was using TASO to raise money and divert it to UWCM?

Respectfully and patiently, Edith explained that she wanted to reach *all* women, churched or unchurched, including the unmarried. Not all women who attend church are legally married; many are second or third wives. And not every church had a MU branch. Edith had to take Andrew, her driver, to speak for her at some men-only church meetings where women weren't allowed. This went against the grain, but Edith would rather bend to tradition than put her work in jeopardy. And Andrew was a good friend who made sure her message got through. Later this attitude softened, and Edith could send other advocates, both male and female, to speak on her behalf.

Eriasa lived only a stone's throw away from Edith's office. When a UWCM team visited him on Easter Monday and found his emaciated form on a mat outside his cottage, he struggled to sit upright to tell his story. Eriasa caught AIDS while he was in the army. His wife had died, leaving him with two daughters aged five and seven. UWCM persuaded him to have an AIDS test. On hearing that he was HIV+ Eriasa said, 'I was stunned. In a split second I relived my wasted life and contemplated suicide.' The team counselled him, fed him and paid his medical bills. But Edith recognised another need: as a Muslim, Eriasa would find it easier to confide in a man. So she and David visited him together. Eriasa was puzzled. Why should these Christians do all this for him? They explained that for them, creed was no barrier to compassion. Eriasa loved talking to David and hearing stories from the bible. David's favourite was from Matthew Chapter 25 about the sheep and the goats, especially verse 40: *'I tell you the truth, whatever you did for one of the least of these brothers of mine, you did for me.'*

Just before he died Eriasa told them, 'I have found it, the eternal life through Jesus Christ. I felt so much joy in my heart knowing that Christ loves and has forgiven me of my past life.' He asked for the gospel to be preached at his funeral. The Muslim community were furious, but Eriasa told them, 'I'm mature, and nobody told me to become a Muslim. Now I choose to become a Christian. When I was sick no Muslim came near me, but these Christian women helped me. I'm leaving my two daughters in their care, and I want them to become Christians, too.' Eriasa made a will, and his sister became his daughters' caretaker. For his baptism he chose the Christian name of Patrick. After his death on 28 April, David and Edith took his girls to church for baptism, giving them the new names of Bessie and Martha.

In May the Navigators, an evangelistic group in America, sent four girls and four boys, high school students, with a married couple of teachers, to spend a month of their school holidays with UWCM. Working with the community, these young Americans completed plastering and flooring Faith House. They carried sand and cement and bought shutters, glass and paint out of their own funds. But this was their school holiday, and they deserved a break, so David and Edith hired a minibus and drove them through the verdant foothills of Mount Elgon, to the spectacular Sipi Falls. One girl, who had expected to spend all her time in Uganda amongst the poor in a crowded city, wept when she saw the beauty of the falls and the mountain heights.

Edith was invited to speak at an AIDS conference for NGOs at Windsor in June. Her theme: the effectiveness of HIV/AIDS work in developing countries. She visited Windsor Castle just as some kind of fun event was happening. Edith was thrilled to see antique cars, a man on a monocycle – and the Queen.

While in England, Edith found time for a heart-to-heart with Elizabeth Swarbrick about Solomon's eye. It was not only useless – it was unsightly. Now twenty years old, Solomon was still in pain, and because of his poor sight he'd had to abandon his beloved scientific studies. Edith asked Elizabeth whether something could be done to remove the eye. Elizabeth spoke to her friend Greta Williamson, who had been to Uganda with her. They took Edith to see their GP, whose opinion was that unless the eye was removed, the pain would continue. And Solomon was in danger of becoming totally blind. He would make enquiries about the cost of the operation.

The Consultant Ophthalmologist at Royal Preston Hospital, Mr Mark Talbot, agreed to operate on Solomon without charge at a local private hospital. They in turn offered free treatment. Apart from those at the Moorfields Eye Hospital in London, Mr Talbot was the only surgeon performing a pioneering technique: when an eye is removed the muscles are left intact, allowing the artificial eye to move like a normal eye. Solomon's damaged eye was removed, and a matching eye fitted. Elizabeth and Greta found ways of paying for the lenses and Solomon's flight to England. Now he could get on with his studies, learn to drive, live a normal life and face the future with confidence. His family and friends were thrilled to see the change from withdrawn youngster to confident young man.

Faith House still had no ceiling, so Edith, by now an expert at asking for help, approached the Dutch Embassy. They paid for the materials, chain link security fencing, and a photocopier. Many AIDS clients had married and become pregnant, with shocking consequences for them and their families.

Tearfund had warned Edith that their financial support would be scaled down after the first year. Over five years it was reduced from an initial £30,000 to £8,000 per annum. This left a big gap. Other supporters would give money for specific projects, but allowed only a small percentage for administration.

Finding new staff wasn't a problem; keeping them was. When there was no money to pay them at the end of the month, life became very difficult. Richard Wamembi had been a dedicated, hardworking member of her staff since 1992. He left to do his MA degree, and Edith was bitterly disappointed when afterwards he went to work for World Vision International. However Richard is still a member of her board and helps with networking and fundraising. Betty Mwandha took over as Programmes Co-ordinator.

Besides his constant support for Edith's work, David had his own projects. CCP had grown over the years and now needed a committee to run it. And not all committee members shared David's vision and personal commitment. Misunderstandings led to disagreements, and then to personal clashes. All this was totally foreign to David's nature, and the time came when he could bear it no longer. CCP, his brain (and heart) child, was being forced out of his hands. Distraught, David had to be hospitalised more than once. Diabetes and malaria affected his general health. Edith and the children found this hard to bear. 'His heart was broken,' foster-daughter Janet said, 'and we were all heartbroken for him.' It would take them some time to restore David to his optimistic, energetic self.

In October Edith returned to the UK for another meeting of non-church NGOs, including TASO.

A newsletter in December 1995 reported much that was hopeful. Needy children were being sponsored in schools. Clients praised UWCM for the practical help they'd been given in will-writing and standing up for their rights. Forty pigs had been given to over twenty families, and ten of those pigs were due to farrow in January 1996. Edith said, 'Soon the families will be in a position to participate in their children's education through income generated from selling these pigs. This certainly will go a long way in reducing heavy reliance on UWCM.' A teenage orphan who'd never been to school was being trained in piggery management, and Edith intended to take on four more apprentices the following year. Her vision was for all five to be equipped to run their own piggery projects. In the meantime UWCM would launch a new commercial venture – sausage making and a pork butchery. Edith was very excited about this new venture.

But her excitement was short-lived. After this newsletter went to print there was an outbreak of Swine Fever. The District Veterinary officer advised Edith to sell off the remaining stock, disinfect the premises, and re-stock six months later. She dealt with her disappointment by spending the proceeds of the sale on an in-calf heifer. Although UWCM broke even financially, they were still sad to lose their prize-winning animals.

There were other sad notes. Only seventeen CCH had been active, the rest hampered by lack of funds and transport. Of the forty original AIDS clients, twenty-nine had died. Lack of funds also meant that there wouldn't be another newsletter until December 1996, and no Children's Conference for many years for the same reason. But when the President of Uganda, Yoweri Museveni came to open the new offices in 1996, UWCM had much to be proud of.

CHAPTER 21

1996-7 ~ the President calls, but the pressures increase

On 16 February 1996 the office was abuzz with excitement. His Excellency Yoweri Kaguta Museveni, President of Uganda, had graciously agreed to open UWCM's new offices. The staff of six pushed all other work aside and prepared for a state visit. Flags and bunting, food and drinks had to be found, new clothes bought or old ones mended, washed and pressed.

Edith made a special visit to Beatrice, her dressmaker in Mbale High Street. Beatrice had fitted Edith out for other special events, but this would be the most important so far. The traditional Uganda dress was beginning to disappear from the streets of Kampala, but the further one travelled away from the capital, the more often it was seen. Every dress is identical in style, so the choice of fabric and colour is all-important. In rich colours with the right earrings and necklace, the effect can be dramatic. So Edith was very particular about her choice of colours for the big day. From the hundreds of fabrics packed into Beatrice's cramped little shop, she chose a very feminine purple and gold floral silk, but topped it with it a military style white peaked cap. All her staff wore the same caps.

Edith had taken it for granted that the police and the President's bodyguards would take care of security. What she hadn't bargained for was a thorough search of their home and office twenty-four hours in advance, and having to bed and feed twelve security men behind locked doors overnight. But they'd coped with all those refugees for three years, so they could cope with this. In any case, they had no choice.

February was a good time for the visit. The roads were still dry and passable. Later they would be choked with mud. This is the time for digging and planting seeds before the March and April rains. But today there was little digging going on. Hundreds of excited people lined the roads, wearing their Sunday best and waving the Ugandan flag with its bird symbol, the Crested Crane. (Edith has her own interpretation of the colours of the flag: black for living in the dark, gold for light shining in the darkness, and red for the blood of Christ.)

Sixteen children waited outside the gates of the compound wearing white caps like Edith's. One little girl clutched a bunch of flowers to present to His Excellency, others held placards reading: 'Defend the Orphan', 'Reach the Orphan', 'Counsel the Orphan', 'Console the Orphan' and 'Direct the Orphan'. All the VIPs stayed cool and comfortable under an awning, but every other inch of the Faith House compound was crowded.

When the President's Landrover was sighted at 11 a.m. a great roar and ululation filled the air. The President stepped out, smart but informal in khaki slacks, short-sleeved shirt and bush hat. After a formal welcome he was introduced to the special guests, then to Edith's staff. It was one of the proudest moments of Edith's life when the President spoke of his admiration for her work and that of her team. He cut the ribbon, then stepped over the threshold of Faith House.

After a display of music and dance by the women, the President was shown around the compound. He declined Edith's invitation to inspect the piggery, now cleaned, disinfected and ready for restocking. He was more interested in their two heifers. Both had calved and were giving 10 litres of milk per day, which helped to pay secondary school fees for five or more orphans. Edith was proud of this pair, but the President wasn't impressed. 'They're not very good specimens, are they? I'll send you a better pair, some pure breed.' And he did.

As graciously as he had arrived, the President left. There was much clearing up and putting away to be done, but it had all been worthwhile. The UWCM was now officially commissioned and nationally recognised.

Three months later President Yoweri Museveni was re-elected with a 75% majority. But there was still support for his opponents in the north, and fighting continued there.

The piggery was restocked, the boar and sow quickly reproduced, and Edith reported: 'UNDP has promised to buy for us hand-processing machines for sausages and we are looking forward to receiving them. They also facilitated us with a Vocational Skills Development Centre at Bungokho for out-of-school youths. Two girls and eight boys are training in carpentry and joinery. Through the Trickle-Up Programme we have funded twenty families for small income-generating projects. We are grateful to the Trickle-Up Programme for the growing partnership with UWCM. Friends from Clevedon donated two electric typewriters, a slide projector, four second-hand sewing machines and lengths of fabric. These will go a long way to improve our work. We are grateful.'

Edith never turned down an opportunity for more training. Her file of certificates shows three day courses in April and October covering HIV/AIDS prevention, with emphasis on planning and finance management, and a further three days with British Council in Entebbe in October on NGO management.

In a letter to friends at the end of 1996 David reported: 'Edith and I have continued with our marriage counselling ministry both with individual and public teaching in YWAM and Church seminars. There is so much need we have observed and many times we feel like spending more of our time in this area.'

When Jim and Sydney Sparling, Edith's Canadian friends, visited that year, she took them to meet Sarah Watundu (Ch 19) at Sakiya. Jim recognised signs of malnutrition in most of the children, and knew the difference even one extra weekly feed could make. They got down to practical details, and the Sakiya Porridge and Prayer Club was born. Sarah told Jim and Sydney that on rainy days they all had to huddle beneath one leaky roof. Her work was frustrated by lack of space and money. With the help of their church in Canada, Jim and Sydney helped to fund the scheme, starting with a hundred big, brightly-coloured plastic mugs, and the cost of the porridge. Once a week the children would meet for fun and Christian teaching – and a mug of porridge. The main ingredient would be millet, supplemented by milk, honey or sugar, or whatever extras came to hand.

Sarah's Pastor helped her to form a committee, all trained in First Aid, using whatever simple AIDS came to hand, such as Aspirin and oral rehydration mixture. Armed with rubber gloves, tea and porridge, they visited homes twice a week, cleaning and feeding. When a parent died, they taught their families to carry on. The initial disdain for porridge was quickly overcome.

In October Edith and Christine flew to Johannesburg, two of twenty Ugandan women on their way to the seventh AGM of the Pan African Christian Women's Association. Men had been invited from West Africa, Tanzania, Malawi, America and the USA, and David was there to represent AEE. The aim was to bring churches and evangelical organisations together internationally. They were cautioned not to leave the compound after dark. But they did venture out to the markets to buy presents for the children.

Back in Uganda the truck, two motorbikes and six bicycles from England were being put to good use. A generous donation from UNDP helped to support seven women's groups in their income-generating activities. Save the Children Norway set up child advocacy and participation programmes and village committees trained in child welfare, HIV/AIDS education and life skills. They supported 180 orphans with education, and equipped ten youths with carpentry skills. By 1996 child sponsorship had increased to 226, supported by the UNDP for one year.

In Christmas week Edith brought together thirty-four people with AIDS. The theme of the day: 'One hope, one world', emphasising the need to stop the spread of AIDS, think positively and make plans for their families. But many were too sick to attend. One had been beaten up by people envious of the help she'd received. Another had died leaving her five children starving.

Early in 1997 a visitor from Clevedon, North Somerset, found eight thriving women's groups supported by UWCM. She reported back:

- **Wabukhasa Tubana.** Wabukhasa means 'a difficult place'. The UNDP had financed a group of lock-up shops which could be rented. With small loans members were starting small businesses, including tailoring, hairdressing, knitting and crochet.

- **Bubulo Tubana** gave mutual financial and practical help, swapping ideas on homecare, cooking and handicrafts. UWCM had given them two heifers, and the calves had been passed on, providing manure and milk both for sale and consumption.
- **Namindambo**. After a shaky start in 1993 this group learned new skills from other groups. UWCM counsellors met their members regularly and helped individuals.
- **Bunaporo**. The aim of this group of twenty-five in a wet forest area was to boost the women's incomes, assist the disabled and orphans, promote health and increase their nutritional skills. They too had a pair of heifers from UWCM, and promoted poultry and bee-keeping as well as learning new crafts.
- **Gangam**a. Twelve women organised craft, poultry, pigs, tree-planting and brick-making schemes. They wanted to add tailoring to the list but there was insufficient money. They also ran a school for orphans.
- **Makargo**, a new group near the Kenya border, was eager to learn about health, nutrition, cooking, poultry rearing, farm management and agriculture. They wanted to raise money for a sewing machine and livestock. UWCM was helping them to fulfil all these aspirations.
- **Shisinyo**. The word means 'an isolated place surrounded by rivers'. This well-organised group of forty wasn't far from UWCM headquarters, but when a strategic bridge was washed out it meant a long detour. The nearest health centre was far away, and the Health Aid Post they set up gave badly-needed help. But they couldn't afford to pay a nurse and often ran out of drugs. One of the donated bicycles helps their counsellor to reach women with HIV/AIDS.
- **Busiita** was an hour's drive from UWCM, in a beautiful but isolated spot near Mount Elgon. The only bridge was often closed by the heavy rains. The thirty-member United Women's Group exchanged ideas about crafts and cookery and supplemented their incomes by selling milk and eggs from the heifer, six goats and

poultry provided through UWCM.

Edith visited a Muslim widow whose husband had died of AIDS during the war. Three of her sons also had AIDS, and she was left with five grandchildren. She had to walk six miles a day to cultivate her small plot of land to feed them. When her house was burnt down every possession, every scrap of clothing was gone. UWCM helped to put a roof over her head and feed her and the children. Most important, they gave her some hope for the future. She told Edith she had felt that God had never loved her, and found it hard to understand why Christian women should care for her. David and Edith enabled another widow dying of AIDS to make a will, ensuring that her daughters would not be left homeless and penniless. Without it her brother would have grabbed whatever property she left.

In September 1997, medical people from all over the world attended the second international conference of the Association of Hospice and Palliative Care at the Royal College of Physicians in London, and Edith was invited to speak about her work. Elizabeth Swarbrick remembers: 'Edith made a great impression, not only because of her knowledge and presentation, but also her humility. The Chairman invited Edith to sit at the top table and offer the Grace before dinner. Edith was thrilled that her Christian faith was recognised, and she could pray with and for all those present.'

While in the UK, Edith visited Bridget Withell in Kent. When Bridget told Edith she was looking for a dissertation topic for her nursing degree, Edith urged her, 'Come and write about my ladies.' The following October she stayed with David and Edith for a month of research.

The UNDP closed their programme to combat HIV/AIDS in 1997, but UWCM was one of three organisations in the Mbale area they nominated to work as 'umbrella' organisations. They were given £50,000 for their own use and to oversee the work of seven other NGOs. The Ministry of Health gave help under their Sexually Transmitted Infections projects.

A newsletter in May 1998 listed items to be thankful for: a new vehicle donated by Tearfund and six bicycles donated by the Ministry of Health for their CCH. Five sewing machines were already in use, and fourteen more were expected soon. And the sausage machine had arrived.

David returned to work after being hospitalised twice with diabetes and malaria, but was still not well.

The huge problem of paying professional staff was never ending, and the pressure of work was building up. All were working flat out. Some months Edith didn't know how their wages would be paid. Young Christian professionals would join UWCM with high hopes, work with enthusiasm for a while, and then have to face the reality of rents to be paid and families to be fed and educated. One by one they found work elsewhere. Their Receptionist, Betty, was in hospital with HIV/AIDS. Edith wrote to her friends: 'This has been very painful for us as a UWCM family because we've always cared for others outside, but found it difficult within the organisation. Betty is a single mother with five children and we don't know how to handle this. Please pray for us.' Betty died of AIDS.

Most hurtful was the fact that some left only after Edith had spent precious time training them. And whenever this happened, Edith was the one carry the burden of extra work, as well as her own. In the years to come this nightmare often made both David and Edith ill with distress.

CHAPTER 22

1998 ~ the First Lady visits. Edith goes to New York

The President may not have been impressed by Edith's piggery, but someone else was. Above Sam Jamie Ibanda's desk in his Kampala office is a framed text:

'The man on his knees to God can stand up to anything.'

Since September 1994 Sam Ibanda had been a programme officer for HIV/AIDS work in Uganda, setting up branches in Fort Portal and Mbale. While he was designing major programmes, Sam took on board some of the small local organisations already in place. UWCM was one of them. He made several visits to monitor their work and was impressed by what he saw, especially the piggery programme.

One morning early in 1998 Sam found a letter on his desk from UNDP headquarters in New York. It was from the Advisory Committee for the International Day for the Eradication of Poverty. The notepaper was impressive: Secretary General: Kofi Annan, Chairman: Danny Glover (the actor), UNDP Goodwill Ambassador, Co-chairs: Mrs Nane Annan, James Gustave Speth (Admin. UNDP) and the actor Harry Belafonte.

The letter explained that every year the UN gives awards to people whose work has made an impact on poverty, and Sam was asked to nominate someone for this year's award. There were only two criteria: it must be a woman, and she must be making a difference to lives, especially of women, the vulnerable and the disadvantaged. The award was to be presented in New York on 17 October that year.

Sam remembers, 'My team of co-ordinators unanimously agreed that UWCM, and especially their Director, deserved to be nominated. When we looked at the work of UWCM, especially Edith, we were convinced that they fulfilled this second criterion. I knew her work, and I knew how dedicated Edith was. I wrote a single page justification and took this to the Minister of Finance. The Minister had selected one other candidate and sent both names to the UN Secretary General's office in New York.'

In June Sam telephoned Edith and told her he was putting her name forward to the UN for an award. He asked her to send him her life history, education etc. Two weeks later he rang again: a film crew would be coming from New York to film the work of UWCM. A team of six, including some from Uganda TV, spent a week going from community to community and recording UWCM's work.

That month the annual Mbale District Show was held at the town's cricket ground, and Edith and Esther were manning the UWCM information stall when Kofi Annan strolled up and greeted them all warmly. Esther had replaced Betty as Women's Programmes Officer, and was thrilled to be introduced in this capacity *and* as Edith's foster-daughter. Mr Annan told Edith how much he appreciated the support given to people at grassroots level, and to the government. She was helping them all to have a better understanding of the problems; he encouraged her to continue in this development work.

When the President's wife heard about Edith, she wanted to see this phenomenon for herself. Edith would have been happy simply to pick up the phone and invite her, but she was cautioned that the correct protocol must be followed. First she must approach the district leaders about sending an invitation. In any case, the First Lady would be too busy. But the First Lady persisted. And so did Edith. Mrs Janet Museveni accepted Edith's formal invitation, and popped in for a visit later in June. Her arrival created almost as much excitement as her husband's had done. Once again UWCM's offices were decked with flags and a celebration cake was iced. A small cavalcade drove into the UWCM compound, and Mrs Museveni stepped out of the white Mercedes, tall, slim and elegant, in a white and black dress trimmed with splashes of bright orange.

But Mrs Museveni wasn't there simply to cut a ribbon and give a blessing. Edith took her to the homes of two families supported by UWCM, both of widows caring for orphaned grandchildren. Outside each house, as the custom is, Mrs Museveni sat on a folding chair and talked to the widows.

The first was Jesska, whose story has already been told. Woman to woman, she told Mrs Museveni that meeting Edith had been the turning point in her life.

The other was Mary Mutenyo, who had a similar story to tell. Eight years earlier she was widowed with six children. Her husband's family accused her of killing their son, and grabbed whatever property he had left. Outraged, Mary's only thought was to infect as many as possible, then kill herself and the children. Then UWCM intervened. With their help she started to buy and sell vegetables. The profits paid for a bicycle, enabling her to travel to the wholesalers and expand her market. Her next venture was to rear chickens, which she exchanged for a goat. The goat produced twins and triplets, and soon she had her own 'bank of goats', as she called them. She exchanged these for a cow, and later sold this to buy land. (Mary died in 2004, but left her children grown up and independent.)

Mrs Museveni listened quietly to other heartbreaking stories of children dying of AIDS, and the women's struggle to bring up young children with no cash and few resources. She heard how UWCM had helped: houses had been repaired, children clothed and school fees paid. Best of all, they'd been given friendship and hope. Back in Faith House she talked to representatives of the women's groups, then she cut into that cake and had a cup of tea before leaving. Her visit was invaluable in raising the profile of UWCM.

A month later Edith received a five-minute summary of UN's week of filming; she had been chosen. In September UNDP took her passport and arranged a visa. Sam remembers, 'We felt lucky as a country when Edith was selected for that award, and facilitated her travel to New York.' She was given a business class air ticket and $2000 for expenses.

Edith made another crucial visit to Beatrice, her dressmaker. The fabric she chose this time was taffeta, with stripes of dark blue, red and gold. The effect was dignified, even regal.

Geoff Cargill had been a keen Tearfund overseas volunteer. When he died of a heart attack his young widow, Shirley, was determined to continue his work. She heard of UWCM and wrote to Edith in 1998. Was there was anything she could do to help? Edith replied, 'We've been given some second-hand sewing machines. Come and teach our ladies some income-generating skills, like dressmaking or knitting.' Shirley flew to Uganda at her own expense, armed with simple dressmaking patterns and a bundle of knitting needles. But on reaching Faith House she found those sewing machines still in their boxes: no-one had been able to spare the time even to unpack them.

Shirley's first job, with a screwdriver and a bit of cannibalisation, was to get those machines, some without spools and all out of tension, fit for use. Andrew then drove her out to the villages and the machines were distributed. The women were eager to learn, but Shirley hadn't realised that most of the things taken for granted in even the poorest western home – a table, sewing thread, a few pins and a pair of scissors – were luxuries here. Many of the women she was teaching to knit were actually good at crochet, something she'd never learnt. Shirley found the relaxed local attitude to time disconcerting at first. She would turn up for a two o'clock meeting to find no-one in sight, but came to admire the determination of the thirty or forty who turned up late after walking many miles, sometimes in defiance of their husbands' objections.

It was disconcerting, too, to talk to the some of those husbands. Their wives were afraid to take the pill, and as they wanted many children they wouldn't use a condom. Shirley asked, 'Aren't you interested in getting rid of AIDS?' and was shocked to be told, 'Not particularly.'

Shirley was leaving just as Bridget Withell arrived. To study the effects of bereavement on women, Bridget went into the villages and talked to them. Women who were HIV+ talked freely to her about the smallest detail of their lives. Esther often had to translate for her. Perhaps the biggest shock for was to be told by one woman that becoming HIV+ was the best thing that ever happened to her: as her old life fell apart, a new one had begun. With Edith's help she was able to face the future as a valued individual, making her own choices for the first time in her life.

Bridget made some fascinating, sometimes disturbing, discoveries. She was taken to Introductions, weddings and funerals. The

Introduction, for instance, is a time for rejoicing as well as business. The bridegroom's family pay the dowry, and the bride's family pay for a big feast. The groom also pays for the wedding. Once the gifts have been given and officially accepted, it's time for fun and rejoicing. There's a game of hide-and-seek, where the groom has to pick out his bride, hidden behind all the other girls. Once he's found the right one, he gives her a flower, and she places a garland around his neck.

Bridget was puzzled, first at one wedding, then another, to see dozens of baby girls and toddlers in frilly dresses, but no boys. 'Where are all the boys?' she whispered to Esther. 'Half of those *are* boys,' Esther replied. 'They just like to dress them that way.'

At one funeral Bridget was distressed to see concrete being mixed in a wheelbarrow alongside the grave, then poured over the body as soon as it had been lowered. This practice probably ensures that the body can't be dug up by wild animals, a real danger with scavengers such as hyenas never far away.

A woman's body is usually buried at her parents' home. Esther took Bridget to the funeral of a client who had died of AIDS. Her husband, himself HIV+, had spent every last penny on medical bills. But when he arrived with his wife's body, her parents demanded money for goats before they would bury her. Bridget was horrified. 'This is terrible,' she whispered to Esther. 'How can they be so mercenary at a time like this, in front of her husband and children?' Esther was quite calm. 'They're not being mercenary. It's a question of their daughter's honour. She went to him without a dowry. Now they need to know that she was of some value, or they'll be ashamed for her.' Somehow Esther managed to find the money needed to settle the matter.

It's part of everyday village life for the men to sit in a circular shelter around a big clay pot of *busera*, all drinking from it with bamboo straws. Here they discuss the problems of the world, and get drunk. Bridget could smell the strong-smelling brew as she walked past, and knew what disastrous effects an impure brew could cause.

On 10 October Edith went to town to have her hair done. The next day David, Edith and Bridget drove to Kampala. After they'd visited Christopher at his school, they went to the newly-opened Mildmay Clinic, where Stephen Watiti was working. There was a farewell party before Edith left on the evening flight to Nairobi.

There was a big welcome at Kennedy Airport for Edith and four other women from France, Jordan, India and the Dominican Republic. They were taken to the UN Stanza Hotel. The following morning a fleet of five cars arrived, each with a guard, to take them to Kofi Annan's house for breakfast, arriving at 8 a.m. precisely. Mr Annan wasn't at home, but they were greeted by his wife. Edith had to fight back the tears as she soaked up the warmth and grace of her welcome, and the grandeur of the surroundings. Edith thought, 'Who am I, that I could even come close to Kofi Annan and go to his house and sit at his table? It looked a mystery, but that's what the Lord can do. Praise the Lord!' In this she was echoing the words of Psalm 113: *'He raises the poor from the dust, He lifts the needy from the dunghill to give them a place among princes, among princes of His people.'* Fifteen sat down at a big table for breakfast, with one waiter for each person.

After breakfast they were driven to the United Nations offices to have their photographs taken and their acceptance speeches checked and rehearsed.

Before the awards ceremony there was a showing of the film '*Beloved*', from the novel by Toni Morrison, who had won the Nobel Prize for Literature in 1993. The story, about a woman's fight against slavery, was appropriate. Edith wasn't sure which gave her a bigger thrill – sitting next to Kofi Annan to watch the film, or meeting the stars, Oprah Winfrey and Danny Glover, afterwards. The two-hour programme included music and dance. The Vice-President of Uganda, Mr Spezioza Kazibwe, was also there.

One by one the five women were called forward. A video of their work was shown, and each was presented with a Certificate of Recognition. A photograph shows Mr Kofi Annan smiling as Mr Gustave Speth of the UNDP presents Edith with a certificate:

'to commemorate the International Day for the Eradication of Poverty presented to Edith Wakumire for her achievements, courage and inspiration in contributing to the fight against poverty.'

In her acceptance speech, Edith called this award 'a much-needed shot of adrenaline that will help increase our speed in the race against poverty.'

The rest of the time was packed with meeting leaders in the UN office, World Food and other NGOs.

On the fourth day, with three days still to go, Edith was horrified to find that her hotel bill had already devoured most of her $2000 expenses. She contacted an American friend who'd once stayed with her and David, a member of 'Trickle Up', part of the Billy Graham organisation. The friend invited Edith into her home for the remaining three days, and took her to see the White House, the Twin Towers site and the UN Assembly Hall.

Before flying home Edith spent a week in Florida with Christine's son.

Back home in Kampala, the Welcome Home party at Parliament House was shown on TV. In a BBC interview Edith said, 'I wish this award was shared by every person who contributed because it was not me – it was all of us.' Back in Mbale, her staff had invited many local dignitaries to another grand party. Edith told Bridget Withell in a letter, 'There were ululations all over coupled with singing and dancing as I was welcomed in the conference hall. You needed to be around to witness this.'

In December David's diabetes forced him to retire.

The timing of Edith's award was critical. By the following year UNDP funds were so low that they could no longer support programmes as they'd done in the past. Edith protested to her friend Sam Ibanda that by sending volunteers into the communities for follow-up work, UWCM's was still fighting against HIV/AIDS. He agreed with her, but there was nothing more he could do.

CHAPTER 23

1999 ~ the Silver Wedding. Community Mobilisation Teams established

While Edith was more and more in demand outside Uganda, visitors from all over the world were now flocking to visit UWCM. Edith's diary for 1999 was daunting. In March alone there were visits from Elizabeth Swarbrick and Joy and Ray Thomas before Edith left for a Tearfund international consultation in Limuru, Kenya.

But her biggest date was with David in May. *'Speak up for those who cannot speak for themselves, for the rights of all who are destitute. Speak up and judge fairly; defend the rights of the poor and needy.'* (Proverbs 31:8&9). David had always connected those words with Edith's work. But the rest of the chapter he applied to her personally. *'A wife of noble character who can find? She is worth far more than rubies. Her husband has full confidence in her and lacks nothing of value. She brings him good, not harm, all the days of her life.'* (vv 10-12).

On 4 May 1999 this 'wonder couple', as they came to be known, returned to Nabumali High School and walked down the aisle of St Peter's Chapel to celebrate their Silver Wedding with a renewal of their wedding vows. Beatrice had done her proud once again with a purple and silver lace bridal gown, allowing for Edith's now more generous proportions. (Her love of food had taken its toll over the years.)

Nabumali High School had grown out of all recognition since David and Edith's day. There were 500 students when they left; now there were 1,600.

They were overjoyed that Stephen, although still very weak, was able to join them. Photographs show them cutting a wedding cake in the school dining room, as proud and thrilled as any newlyweds. The big difference was that any remnants of shyness had disappeared. These were two mature Christians who had loved and trusted each other for twenty five years. And together they trusted God with whatever the future might bring. Edith called David her 'silver boy'.

In June Edith received a letter from Danny Glover, UNDP Goodwill Ambassador and Co-Chair of the Poverty Eradication Advisory Committee, telling her that she'd been elected as a member of that committee.

Later that year Edith had an excited phone call from the Sheraton Hotel, Kampala, where her second foster-son, Paul, was a Manager. 'Guess what, Mum – this week I'm supervising a dinner for President Clinton!'

Since his mother died when he was fifteen, Paul had regarded David and Edith as Mum and Dad. After a catering course Paul had worked at the Sheraton Hotel in Kampala, then for two years at the Qatar Embassy Hotel. On his return to Kampala he was promoted to management. Now he'd been given this special job: look after Bill Clinton, his wife and their four guests.

Two of Paul's great assets were his natural courtesy and easy, confident manner. Bill Clinton congratulated him on the meal and asked Paul about his work. Paul found the President very easy to talk to, and repeated their conversation to Edith word-for-word. She was always delighted to hear from Paul, who'd caused her far less anxiety than some of her other children.

Edith wrote in an official 1999 report: 'Disaster befell people of Bushika-Manjiya county in Eastern Mbale on Monday 30 August 1999 at 1.00 p.m. when landslides disrupted the set order. Eighteen people were confirmed dead and two injured while several houses, household property, crops and land were washed down the slopes. Four orphans supported by UWCM were greatly affected when their banana and coffee plantations were destroyed. Their hut is in a very dangerous location and UWCM is helping the boys construct another house in the lower parts of the area. The Ministry responded with foodstuffs, clothing, bedding and some financial assistance. Collections are still being made by the church and well-wishers in the community alongside government intervention to arrest the crisis.'

The report went on: three hundred people were homeless, including eight families supported by UWCM. Their help included iron sheets, nails and skilled labour. The poorest forty families were given small grants to run a business with the help of 'Trickle-up', including training in simple record keeping. (UWCM insists that children be included in all decision-making.)

Ben, an orphan who'd been helped through secondary school, was now a music teacher, able to take care of his siblings. Fourteen girls and ten boys were in their first term of secondary school. But UWCM couldn't afford the £360 per term one young person needed to stay at university.

Between April and September, thirty volunteers had made 434 visits to the sick. Over twenty clients had died and ten were very ill. But as the work expanded, Edith saw that by working as a team women could work more efficiently. So she organised these thirty into a Community Mobilisation Team (CMT). Each Community Counselling Helper (CCH) made a personal commitment to spend two days a week helping five families.

Three more CMT were formed in the next few months – an astonishing total of 120 CCH. They were the basis for income-generating schemes. UWCM would give a starter, for example a goat, to fifteen of the women, who would hand the resulting kids on to the other fifteen. Further kids would be passed on to orphans and other needy people, each family benefiting from the milk as their goats matured. Other groups might start with a cow, poultry or bees.

When Agatha's husband was moved to Kampala Agatha, with all her accounting skills, went with him. But four other good workers were found.

With the help of Norway's Save the Children in Uganda, UWCM launched a new venture: the Child Rights Clubs. Thousands of children had been left with the job of bringing up their younger siblings. Malnutrition and poor access to education had always been the norm: now children were more vulnerable than ever. With no protector in the house, many girls were exposed to rape. They were left with two choices – early marriage or prostitution. Boys became aimless and angry. These clubs taught the rights and responsibilities of children, developed their education skills, and taught about HIV/AIDS. Out-of-work youth were trained in vocational skills through community collaboration. This help from Norway continued until 2006, but the work still goes on through the churches.

At a Judas Trust 'Rivers of Life' international conference in Uganda in November/December 1999, Edith spoke about the link between HIV/AIDS and poverty. She taught how it has especially impacted women and girl children, and how God can intervene.

Edith challenged the bishops present, 'Who in this House of Bishops represents women?', to which the all-male answer was, 'We do.' Her second question was, 'How is the church tackling the care of women? Men and women are made equally in the image of God, in every way equal in value and status. How many of you have made a will leaving an inheritance to your daughters?'

Not a single hand was raised.

'Please speak about this in the churches. And I believe it is right that there should be women Bishops. After all there are women MPs, and every district has a Woman Member of Parliament as well as an elected general constituency MP.'

The bishops nodded in agreement. Then the Archbishop spoke. 'As soon as I get home from this conference, I will write a will to ensure that my wife and daughters will have equal inheritance with my sons.'

A delegate from South Africa, Carla van der Kooinj, reinforced Edith's message about the effect of the disease on children, and told the story of Moses in the bullrushes to show how God can save little children.

Carla, a Dutch woman working with YWAM, had started a home in Brazil for children with HIV/AIDS, and was arranging an international conference for people going to developing countries with YWAM. (Members of YWAM first undergo weeks of discipleship training, then more practical training before they are sent out to work in the world's needy communities.) She asked Edith to be one of her speakers, teaching about the relationship between HIV/AIDS and African culture. Edith didn't hesitate; she pencilled a date for Brazil in her 2000 diary.

The *New Vision* newspaper reported on 15 November 1999 that fifteen women from Uganda had flown to Washington DC for a week's conference on equality and justice for women, its main theme: leadership and decision making.

But the *New Vision* hadn't heard Edith's personal side of the story – a repeat of Christine's 1986 travel disaster. At Entebbe airport she presented her tickets and passport.

'I can't see your UK visa.'

'I'm not going to the UK. I'm going to Washington DC.'

'But you're changing planes at London Heathrow.'

'Yes, but I'm not stepping outside the airport. And besides, I didn't need one last time. I changed at Brussels without one.'

'That was Belgium. You don't need a visa for Belgium. You do for the UK.'

So the rest of the party went on without her, and Edith spent the next two days in Kampala obtaining a UK visa. When she arrived her room at the Washington Plaza Hotel was no longer vacant, and she had to share a room. Edith was upset that she'd missed two days of settling in and bonding. Mrs Museveni had paid for Edith's flight, but the extra costs, including food, were worrying. As Edith remarked later, some things you can only learn the hard way, and checking her own travel arrangements in future was one of them.

CHAPTER 24

2000 ~ a new venture, a further award, and Tamar's wedding

While Tamar was at university she befriended Mary, a girl from South West Uganda. Both graduated with BA Social Science degrees, then Tamar started work at the Italian Embassy while Mary did voluntary work at the Scripture Union office in Kampala. SU offered her a job at their Mbale office, but couldn't afford to pay for her accommodation. Mary discussed her dilemma with Tamar: should she accept the post or shouldn't she? Tamar said she would pray about it. And she did. Then she told her father of Mary's plight. David was SU's regional representative and knew how badly SU needed this valuable young person; there had been no SU staff in Mbale for four years. After he'd talked things over with Edith the inevitable happened – Mary moved in with them. Two months later they rented a house for her. When Mary met a young man, David took part in her Introduction and marriage negotiations. He and Edith were at her wedding in Mbale cathedral.

Mary said later, 'David and Edith showed more love than my own parents ever did. It's wonderful to see their lifestyle. They work as two equal partners. They love God and also his people. I wasn't the only one. Many visitors came, and all got the same warm welcome and care, with lots of smiles and jokes. Edith will never know what an impact she had on my life.'

They had helped Mary, but they couldn't accommodate every working girl in Mbale. Edith's new vision had three aims.

Firstly, a home for vulnerable girls. It was almost impossible for village girls who had been offered work in town to find safe, cheap accommodation.

Secondly, accommodation for paying guests. Hundreds of overseas visitors had stayed in the Wakumire home, others at hotels in Mbale, but the Wakumires' guest wing was always full and many couldn't afford hotel accommodation,

Thirdly, some kind of fund-raising facilities. Edith envisaged that girls who'd been offered cheap accommodation could partly offset this by looking after paying guests.

Edith called this new project the Ebenezer Centre, taking the name from the words of 1 Samuel 7:12: *'Then Samuel took a stone and set it up between Mizpah and Shen. He named it Ebenezer, saying, "Thus far has the Lord helped us."'*

Her friend Bishop Samwiri wrote a foreword to her proposal, she presented it to the Mbale Municipal Council, and the Council approved. It was a proud moment for Edith when the Deputy Mayor, Mrs Hajat Jamilanaleba, signed title deeds on behalf of Mbale Council for 'Two acres for conference facilities and accommodation' on 7 July.

Now came Catch 22: how do you raise funds to build the facilities for a fund-raising project? But the land was theirs, and they had faith in the outcome. Edith asked Bridget Withell and her family in October, 'Please pray for us as we step forward into this big dream.'

In the same letter to Bridget, Edith spoke of another dream. Thanking her for forwarding money for a First Aid kit she says:

'The contribution you have sent through UKET has tremendously bridged the gap especially in emergency cases and in purchasing the drugs for the clients. We get testimonies through the Community Counselling Helpers that this medication has gone a long way to alleviate pains and sicknesses.

'Our idea of the mobile clinic is still on, especially through this First Aid kit. Of course the drugs are few but we still need a part-time Health Worker to follow up the CCH and to treat the bed-ridden patients. However the cost of drugs and meeting the part-time worker is still the problem. Every time such a staff goes out it would cost us 45,000/- per week (£15). But I think that whatever resources we have shall be used as and when available and we shall appreciate this support. If we put up a small mobile clinic, even community people especially children can be treated when the staff go to the village. The nurse can also give health talks.'

This latest dream is still a dream.

On 29 July 2000, David and Edith were in Amsterdam for Billy Graham's third world conference for evangelists. The man himself was in the Mayo Clinic in Rochester, Minnesota, unable to attend, but his place was taken by his son, Franklin. There were 10,000 participants from two hundred countries. The African Children's Choir sang at the opening ceremony, and Sir Cliff Richard sang the Lord's Prayer. Speakers included George Carey, the then Archbishop of Canterbury.

Before the Communion Service on the final day, Billy Graham spoke by video from Minnesota. He said, 'I want to be among those who represent a generation of evangelists that hands the torch to a new generation of God's servants. I believe that the fire of God the Holy Spirit has fallen on this conference and that we have rededicated our lives in a new way to reflect the light of the glory of God. We will go out from Amsterdam with a new fire burning in our hearts to touch a lost world.'

At *Amsterdam 2000* Edith met Samaritan's Purse, an outreach of the Billy Graham organisation promoting help for the poor, and invited them to visit UWCM. In a letter to Terry Game Edith thanked her and her family for their prayers and told them: 'I also had an opportunity to give time for filming about UWCM work by Billy Graham Evangelistic Association Filming Crew. This team followed us to Mbale from 11 to 14 October to film our work in the field for promotional purposes. I am sure the Lord will use such occasion to raise further funding for us.' Samaritan's Purse gave donations to buy a car, and invited her to speak at their Prescription for Hope HIV conference in Washington in 2001.

In August Edith received a puzzling phone call from the Uganda Director of World Vision International (WVI). He told her, 'Every year World Vision International selects two Christians who've contributed to Christian service to people in need. I've been asked for names, and your name has been given to me. I'm sending someone to get your details for the Robert W. Pierce Award.'

Edith had heard Robert Pierce's story. While travelling in China he had found a young homeless girl begging in the street. He gave her US$5, and promised to send her that every month, which he did until he died. Touched by this haunting experience he founded WVI. Edith was puzzled.

'Why me? World Vision has never worked with UWCM.'

'This isn't about organisations. It's about people.'

WVI sent someone to interview Edith, to check on her work and visit some of the communities it had affected, reporting back to their headquarters in Monrovia, California.

But the highlight of family life in 2000 was Tamar's wedding on 23 September. Tamar met Paul Sembiro while she was at Makerere University. Paul was a lecturer in Mechanical Engineering, but was already earning a reputation as a lay preacher. Like David, he was working as a missionary for AEE. David and Edith were overjoyed that Tamar had found a good Christian husband. Bishop Henry Luke Orombi, later Archbishop of Uganda, officiated at the marriage. The Archbishop said later, 'David and Edith produced this wonderful daughter called Tamar, and somehow she brought us even more by marrying this young fellow who matched her so well. It's one of those God-given choices and pairings.' Paul later became Mission Co-ordinator for the Church of Uganda.

At the wedding in St Frances' Chapel, Makerere, the family broke with tradition once again in a small but significant act. When Tamar walked down the aisle in her figure-hugging white lace gown, she was escorted not only by her father but by her mother and three brothers. And when the Minister asked, 'Who gives this woman?' they all replied, 'We do!'

There was one sad echo from their own wedding. On that first occasion David's brother Samson had been dying. This time it was Stephen who was desperately ill with a combination of meningitis, TB and cancer. Tamar had always called Stephen 'my best friend' and she prayed until the very last minute that he would recover in time for her wedding. But he'd been sent home from hospital with a supply of oxygen, and couldn't leave the house. His daughter Deborah, now eleven, was sent to boarding school. Whenever they were in Kampala David and Edith went to see their beloved foster son, whether in Mulago Hospital or at home, and were thankful to see the loving care given to him by people from his church. Edith spent days relieving them of Stephen's day care in hospital. Stephen had three main carers: the housekeeper who had taken care of him and Deborah after her mother died, his sister and a cousin. (Of his cousin Janet Stephen still says 'God bless her!' for the way she bathed him in bed.)

Another joy in 2000 was that Paul announced his engagement to Florence, one of David's CCP protégées.

The National Director of WVI 'phoned Edith in October to tell her she'd been selected. Celebrations were to take place in Kampala in November for the fiftieth anniversary of WVI globally, and their fifteen years in Uganda. David and Edith spent that weekend at the Equatorial Hotel. On 7 November Edith dressed regally once again, and set off for the International Conference Centre. Twenty-two year old Samson, now a university student in Kampala, was with them.

After the formal dinner Edith received a handsome plaque from the hands of Dean Hirsh, the President of WVI, plus a cheque for £5,000 for her work. Her name was added to the large wall plaque in WVI's headquarters in California

In her acceptance speech, Edith said:

'First of all I thank God through His son Jesus Christ for the honour He has bestowed upon me to receive this award. UWCM is an indigenous Christian organisation, committed to serving the poor, valuing people above anything else, stewards of the Lord's resources, which he commits to us through partners, and responsive to the needs in the society. The receiving of this award is a great sign of recognition of our work, which encourages us to do more. However, this comes with its own challenges. The challenges include higher expectations from the communities, more demands on the limited resources and more accountability to the Lord. We therefore request World Vision International, our new partner, to support us in prayer and resources to push us the extra mile.'

She reported that in less than ten years, UWCM had sponsored over four hundred orphaned children. It had trained more than thirty CCH to visit, counsel and care for people infected with HIV/AIDS. It had helped to improve the level of HIV/AIDS awareness. Twenty women's groups had been formed to help other women with education, development skills and access to income-generating projects.

Edith thanked a number of supporters: the District Health services, ActionAid, Save the Children (Norway), Canada Fund, Trickle-up (USA), the Netherlands Embassy, ACET (UK), the UNDP and in particular Tearfund (UK). She ended her talk with the words: 'For God and my country!'

There had been disappointments, but Edith didn't talk about those. The pigs had died of swine fever. Edith's dreams of a sausage-making industry had finally died and that eagerly-awaited sausage machine was still in its box. The cows' udders got sunburnt and they stopped producing milk. But all the goats, cows, apiaries and poultry sent out into the community had thrived and were bringing in bigger incomes. In 1996 UWCM had sponsored 226 children. But they couldn't keep up this high number once the support of Tearfund and UNDP had been phased out. New ways would have to be found to cover the escalating cost of education for orphans. The young man Edith had trained in child counselling left to be Youth Pastor in All Saints Cathedral.

But Edith found other workers. Stephen, a teacher who had worked as Project Director for Compassion for two years, was given the job of Community Facilitator, the focal person for child advocacy, with the emphasis on nutrition and early childhood. That particular project came to an end, but Stephen stayed on in different capacities. That brought the staff up to eleven. And a second CMT had been formed at Nabumali.

Foster-son Paul and Florence were married on 16 December.

Before the end of the year, Stephen Watiti had started his ARV treatment, the first glimmer of light at the end of a long, dark tunnel.

CHAPTER 25

2001-2 ~ Edith to Brazil and Washington, Samson to Cuba

Belo Horizonte, Brazil's third largest city with its sophisticated skyscrapers and fountains, is known as 'the bar capital of Brazil'. But Edith had no time for the usual tourist pursuits: she was there to fulfil her promise to Carla van der Kooinj. However its tropical heat, vegetation (including coffee) and stunning mountain views were very much like those of Uganda, and Edith quickly felt at home there.

There was only one shadow over this big adventure: David's mother, Esther, wasn't well. Mothers-in-law have a reputation for being dragons, but Esther had never been dragon-like. On the contrary, she'd been like a mother to Edith. Her motto had always been, 'work hard and learn a lot.' She worked in her garden every morning and watered it every evening. What she grew, she gave: eggplants, greens, mangoes and bananas were all shared with visitors or the neighbours' children. It wasn't only close family who loved and respected Esther. She would always leave enough at the bottom of the pan to feed a hungry visitor or passer-by. Roast meat and bananas were always put aside for them. Every morning her first visit was to David and Edith. With a knock at their bedroom door she would call out, 'David? How are you? Did you sleep well?' The couple would smile at each other and call out, 'Come in.' She'd tiptoe into the bedroom and sit on a stool, tell them all the latest news, give them some bananas, then go home. But Esther refused to live with them, even when she was unwell.

A few days before Edith left for Brazil, Esther thought she saw someone sitting under the mango tree, and went out for a closer look. She was eighty years old and her eyesight was fading. She didn't see the wire, tripped over it and cracked and dislocated her hip. At her age major surgery was too risky. After a week in hospital she was allowed to mend slowly at home. Esther Nilly, who'd been named after her, moved in, and she and her mother took turns to care for the old lady. A physiotherapist prescribed exercises, but progress was slow. Edith was uneasy as she set off for Brazil.

On 17 April, two days after her arrival, Edith got the phone call she had been dreading: David's mother had died. Her first thought was for David's loss and her own grief, then she realised the predicament she was in: 'But David, I've got a fixed date return ticket, so if I fly home for the funeral I'll have to pay for a single flight. And I'm programmed to teach for five days out of this ten-day seminar and if …'

David stopped her. He had another message for her, this time from her sisters. All four urged her to stay in Brazil. They would do everything necessary. Much later Edith discovered how far-reaching her sisters' help had been. David had never been left alone. They'd taken care of the rest of the family and made all the arrangements for the funeral, including feeding the huge extended family.

At first the neighbours were shocked. Wasn't it her place to do all these things and be alongside her grieving husband? She should have flown home at once. But when they saw the love the sisters had shown, their grumbles turned to murmurs of admiration. They could never have imagined four women leaving home and family for a whole week to do so much for a brother-in-law. Everyone had to admit they'd done a wonderful job. And they had forced another crack in tradition.

In Brazil, Carla and the team offered comfort and support as Edith got on with her valuable work. What she had to say would be important to the twenty-seven young students from the USA, Holland, UK, Canada, Australia and Hawaii. She taught about family life, HIV and AIDS in Uganda, and took the same message to another community of about sixty outside YWAM. It was a relief, on visiting a home for children living with HIV and AIDS, to find them all on ARV and well cared for.

Edith remembers: 'One humbling experience was when the male students washed my feet as a sign of repentance on behalf of African men, who have violated the God-given rights of women, making them more of slaves. They told me they had never before realised how they had exposed women to a deadly disease. They were ashamed. I cried.'

UWCM became a membership body with a joining fee and annual subscriptions, and held its first Annual General Meeting in July. This move widened UWCM's reputation and helped its financial situation a little.

Edith accepted the invitation of Samaritan's Purse and flew to Washington in August for their 'Prescription for Hope' International Christian conference on HIV/AIDS, speaking to the 15,000 delegates about the work of UWCM, and how their women's groups support orphans, vulnerable children and families infected and affected by HIV/AIDS. Edith helped to write the final report and recommendations. There was only one disappointment: Edith was about to show the video of her work made by Samaritan's Purse, when Mrs Museveni turned up and showed one of her own instead. The week of intense work left no time for sightseeing. Edith had to fly home as soon as it ended because David was in hospital with malaria.

Towards the end of September, heavy rains caused landslides in the Mbale and Sironko districts, Cattle rustling in Kenya spilled over into Uganda, hampering some of UWCM's work. But there was a bumper harvest nationally. An estimated 100,000 metric tonnes of maize alone was harvested, and the cost of foodstuffs dropped.

There had been a push to increase the number of CMT and Edith reported:

- **Bumbobi** had collected 300 kgs of maize. They supported 100 orphans and 26 needy people, distributing food and second-hand clothing.
- **Nabumali** had given 500 kgs maize, 150 kgs of beans and some second-hand clothes and shoes. They constructed a house for a needy old widow.
- **Bukhabusi** had collected 517 kgs of maize and 70 kgs of beans
- **Buwalasi** was not yet consolidated. There had been a poor response from the community, and patient follow-up was needed.

Reports from the women's groups were encouraging. The chairman of one group said, 'You have empowered us. We can now dress ourselves and our children. We are able to contribute to their school fees which we could not do before! How shall we thank UWCM for this!' The Chairman of a Local Council added, 'UWCM promises *and* delivers.' The Co-ordinator of another group declared, 'We are overwhelmed by UWCM's commitment to us. We could not believe our eyes when we received the goats. The women are still in a dreamland. They can't believe the goats are theirs and are not going to pay for them except to look after them for their own good.'

One client said of her CCH: 'I would be long dead if this lady had not got me. My husband who did not co-operate died, but I listened to Tolofaina's counsel and that is why I am the way I am. The drugs she gives me are not the same as others that we buy! You take once and the following day you are fine. I can now grow food for my children. When I'm sick I run to my counsellor and my health is improved.'

The drugs UWCM provided were only standard over-the-counter drugs, but it's wonderful what can be done with a couple of Aspirin – and a lot of love.

Education continued to be high on Edith's list of priorities. She and David had struggled to educate their own children, and were always distressed to hear of other cases they couldn't help. Peter, an A-level student, was his grandfather's only carer. When the old man went into hospital, Peter had to wash and feed him every day. Their money ran out. Unable to pay the medical bills, he travelled to Kenya to seek help from his married sister. But she had no money either, not even for Peter's return fare. Three weeks later he got a lift home, but he'd lost a month's schooling. Allan was another senior student who had to tend his mother while she was in Mbale hospital for a month. He could only dash back to school to snatch the odd lesson.

Edith's son Samson had always been a quiet, courteous boy. Even as a small child he'd been a wizard at putting things together, using whatever came to hand such as banana stems and papyrus. David had once been alarmed to find him taking his radio apart, but relieved (and impressed) to see it put together again. When Samson built himself a cart, he harnessed the energy from twenty old batteries to made a headlamp for it. In the final exams at secondary school, Samson was one of the top three, and went on for electrical engineering at Makerere. But there he became complacent, left to take up a computer course, and became an expert at building web sites. Then an advert in the paper caught his attention: scholarships were being offered by the government of Cuba, backed up by the government of Uganda. Samson applied for the course in Electrical Engineering. The Ministry of Education offered to top Cuba's free tuition with 'pocket money', but parents had to pay the two-way fare. David agreed, and sold his Toyota station wagon. But the airline would accept only a single fare for customers spending more than six months at their destination. The Ministry of Education agreed to this, and Samson flew to Cuba in 2002.

CHAPTER 26

2002-3 ~ Edith to Cape Town, then back to University

In 2002 Edith did more church leadership training, and Tamar and Paul presented her with a beautiful, healthy granddaughter, named Esther after her paternal grandmother.

Carla van der Kooinj had set up her ministry through YWAM in Cape Town and urged Edith, 'They've never heard an African woman speak as you do. They need you.' So on 6 October Edith left for South Africa for two weeks, the first of three visits. At the Beautiful Gate School in Cape Town there were seventeen students aged from eighteen to forty-five from the UK, USA, Holland, Zimbabwe, South Africa, Congo and Malawi.

Cape Town was a delightful place for tourists, but disillusioning for a woman from a poor African country. Although apartheid was officially a thing of the past, Edith saw that there was still a big difference between white and black. The only black people she saw in the tourist centres were gatekeepers and entertainers. In Uganda even the poorest had a little land on which to grow food, but from her guest house Edith could see poor, hungry people just sitting and drinking. One night it was very cold, and under her snug bedcovers Edith felt keenly for those outside.

There was still great stigma attached to HIV/AIDS in South Africa. Drunkenness was common, leading to a high incidence of aggression, rape and promiscuity. Edith visited three groups of Africans living with HIV/AIDS. She remembers: 'One group met in a church. At the beginning the church was full, but as time went by without sign of food or handouts, people left one by one until at the end only a few remained. I was told that people would stay only if they were going to be given food. Another group of thirty-two came to the Beautiful Gate and I shared with them about our experience in Uganda. Although they were given the chance to ask questions, not many of them were willing to speak up.' Her message, as always, was one of hope. But her heart sank when her audience listened with heads low, hardly able to look her in the eye. Edith recognised their lack of self-esteem.

Edith paid a sobering visit to Robben Island. She saw the room where Nelson Mandela had been a prisoner for twenty-three years, and marvelled at what he'd endured without breaking his spirit or losing hope.

The next time Edith went to Cape Town she was the only black person in the cable car to Table Mountain. Had apartheid really died, she wondered?

On 12 September 2003 the *Kent Messenger* reported: 'The husband of a talented opera singer who died last year is to hold a charity concert in her memory.' Dorothea Butt and her husband Denis had spent eight years in Uganda. Mr Butt had worked for the Uganda government as an advisor in coffee cultivation. Shortly before she died his wife had decided she wanted to support a charity in Uganda, where all three of their children had been born. She specifically mentioned using it to pay school fees and buy school stationery and uniforms for orphans and needy children, to help child-headed families and to provide seed and livestock. Edith confirmed that the £2,500 was doubly welcome in view of Tearfund's reduced funding. She said, 'Mrs Butt's Memorial Fund will go to support the children in the final year of secondary and Tertiary Institutions. This will give them a future skill so as to support their siblings. Part of the fund will give material support to two child-headed families – with food and basic needs at Christmas.'

Mr Butt had never met Edith, so he was touched to receive a personal letter of thanks from her detailing the help given to specific young people in higher education.

That year Edith's sister Christine dealt with a problem that had long cast a dark shadow over their family life. She sought out Anzerena, the foster mother who'd given them a half-brother. After Chris's birth Anzerena had an ectopic pregnancy and never conceived again. Christine had always regretted the mutual animosity that had scarred their lives. The sisters agreed that a reconciliation was needed. On their behalf Christine begged Anzerena's forgiveness for the way they had despised her as children. And forgave her for any hurt she'd caused them. The two women prayed together, and Christine had the joy of seeing Anzerena give her life to the Lord. But none of them were able to influence Chris. After school he played very little part in their lives.

There was another sign of hope: Stephen Watiti, who had been at the point of death two years earlier, had responded so well to ARV treatment that he was now back at work, although in a limited capacity. He had been commended in a medical journal for his openness in publishing an appraisal of his personal encounter with HIV/AIDS. Once again David and Edith thanked God for this answer to prayer. And through TASO Stephen made a new friend, Naomi, a young widow with four children.

The Christmas 2003 newsletter reported that the reduction in Tearfund support had left many children 'desperate'. Edith pleaded for further support, and gave instances of what sponsorship had achieved. Aida Nafuna, who'd been supported from primary school, had been awarded a B.Ed from Mukono Christian University. Another girl, Annet, who spoke several local languages as well as Kiswahili and English, passed her Uganda Advanced Certificate of Education, then trained as a broadcaster with a local radio station. Edith said, 'We might miss many other graduates among many of the orphaned desperate children.' Of the 185 sponsored children on their books, the future of 176 was now uncertain.

But she added a cheerful note. 'Operation Christmas Child by Samaritan's Purse donated 45 big boxes of gifts to our children. Over 4,000 children in nine rural communities received gifts of shoe boxes. Over 300 children committed their lives to Christ. This was a wonderful tool for reaching children. Children of parents who are living with AIDS in Nkoma said, "We did not know that there are people who love us also. Our neighbours discriminate us that we shall give AIDS to their children. This is because our mothers are HIV positive." This made the visiting team shed tears.'

Another cause for rejoicing was that two more CMT had been

formed, making six in all. After four days of rigorous training each member was given a T-shirt bearing a slogan in the local language. A photograph of one group shows that at least six were male. Their work was continually assessed and supported. They had become a powerful force.

Edith thanked all the organisations and individuals who had helped them. One lady had given all she had, like the old woman in the bible. Edith wrote to her, 'Kathy, your donation will go to family of late Florence who died the day we knew of your donation. She left seven children, the youngest HIV positive. The children have been left under the care of a seventy-four-year-old grandmother and the eldest son who left school to care for the mother while she was sick. He is now taking care of his six siblings. Thank you, Kathy, for this challenging love.'

By 2003 Edith was recognised as an authority on the effects of AIDS on the community and was speaking on the world stage. But she knew that with further qualifications she could speak with even more authority. The business side of UWCM was now enormous. Her Progress and Financial Report for October 2002 to March 2003 filled thirty-nine pages.

After praying for God's guidance, David and Edith discovered she could enrol for a BA Social Work and Administration course without leaving Mbale. So for the next three years, after a hard day's work she would attend evening classes at the Mukono Christian University Study Centre in Mbale, then write out her assignments at home by hand. Her studies included Administrative law, Counselling, Human Resources Management, Industrial Welfare and Demographic and population studies. Working alongside the police, family courts and foster homes, the focus of her field studies was the Probation Officer's work with vulnerable children.

This new venture revealed corners of society deeper and darker than any Edith had ever imagined. One police case in particular shocked her. The eight-year-old girl had always been quiet. Her mother became anxious only when she noticed something awkward about the way her daughter was walking. 'Why are you walking like that?' she asked. 'What's the matter?' 'Nothing,' the child replied. That's what Daddy had told her to say. And in any case, Mummy wouldn't believe her. When her mother did take her to a clinic at last, a cursory examination revealed the extent of the damage. The child needed major surgery to repair or remove her damaged internal organs. Only then did she admit that Daddy had raped her whenever Mummy was out of the house. She would be sterile and incontinent for the rest of her life. The father was jailed. Edith longed to give the child the support and counselling she needed, but mother and daughter left the district without leaving a trace.

Police are mostly concerned with defilement cases, usually reported by observant neighbours. Lost and abandoned children are taken to foster homes, juvenile offenders dealt with in remand homes or rehabilitation and protection units. The authorities work closely with parents and local leaders. But sometimes there's a suspicion, when a local official speaks in defence of a young offender, that a cow or goat has quietly changed hands. The young person may go free, but is left unprotected.

A problem new to Edith is a regular event at the Probation Office. A young girl is impregnated, then left without any help from the father. Only when the child is about five or six – and old enough to work – does the father show any interest. Then he'll claim that his mother will take care of it. If the girl refuses, she may be beaten up. In desperation she turns to the Probation Officer. His main concern is the protection of the child. By law, until a child is five years old it must stay with the mother. The father must provide for both, and has visiting rights. But if the mother has another man in her life, the father doesn't want to feed him as well. And if she has any more children, will they get a share in what he has paid for? So a list of costs is drawn up: milk, rice, meat etc. The Probation Officer has to decide: if a child goes to the father, will the grandmother provide these things? Or (more likely), will it be fed on leftovers? The mother doesn't always offer the best care for her child. If it does go to the grandmother, the mother has visiting rights. Edith was shocked to learn that five or six such cases come to the Probation Office *every day*, especially in the slum suburbs where there is little to eat, and drinking, fighting, overcrowding and promiscuity are common.

These were three years of struggle, but David supported her as he had always donet. He was proud of her. And she kept her eye firmly on the future.

CHAPTER 27

2004-6 ~ the fight against malaria, Edith to Yorkshire and Wales.

The Wakumires gained another 'daughter' in January 2004 when Natasha Edgerton, a tall, athletic young woman from Australia came to live with them for two months. Natasha had completed a Bachelor of Biomedical Science degree, and was now half way through a Masters in Public Health International. Natasha's initial interest was HIV/AIDS, but she soon realised that for the under-fives, malaria was by far the biggest killer. Between 70,000 and 100,000 children in Uganda die of malaria every year. Those leaking roofs and crumbling walls let in mosquitoes as well as rain. There was another hidden danger: a pregnant woman can pick up the parasite without developing malaria. The parasite hides in the placenta, killing or starving her unborn child. Anyone HIV+ is six times more likely to get the disease. Natasha collaborated with women's groups in several villages, designing and carrying out pilot projects in malaria control. Under Natasha's guidance the Local Anti-Malaria Support Programme (LAMPS) was formed.

Natasha had only limited success with her first initiative – the local manufacture of mosquito nets. Even in Kampala she couldn't buy netting cheaply enough. And she certainly couldn't afford to buy it in bulk from Tanzania. Only four nets were produced locally.

But the 'Fight Malaria Day' she organised was a great success. Led by a brass band, hundreds of school children, local people and church members marched to the village hall, where an impressive collection of dignitaries had been invited. A group of women sang a 'Malaria song', then three of the guests spoke on malaria prevention and treatment.

Two of the four nets were donated to two families, the other two auctioned. George Weyamo, a local agriculturalist, briefed the audience on the benefits of the Neem tree as a mosquito repellent, and donated two seedlings to be planted at the church. One of the local councils donated a further five ready-treated mosquito nets.

Natasha's third initiative was the Neem promotion project. Mr Weyamo trained people in the cultivation of the Neem tree, a large tree of Indian origin whose leaves act as a natural insect repellent. Both leaves and seeds can be used in ointment to smear on the skin. But the tree takes five years to mature and seedlings were only available from the unstable Karamoja region, making them difficult to access.

Of David and Edith Natasha says: 'My time with the Wakumire family and in the villages of Mbale was one of the most significant personal experiences of my life. I experienced a profound deeper connection with God and a huge growth in my faith. I was overwhelmed by the amazing sense of faith and relationship with God that they thrive on. At the end of my two months, I felt as though I was being ripped away.'

Natasha's visit overlapped with that of Bridget Withell, allowing the two time to organise a conference for women on health-related topics. They made a good partnership, Natasha concentrating on physical health, Bridget on the psychological effects of illness and bereavement. Both were invited with David and Edith to Namirembe Cathedral, Kampala when the Rt Revd Henry Luke Orombi was ordained as Archbishop of Uganda on 25 January. Perhaps the new Archbishop had Edith in mind when he spoke that day:

'The church has a responsibility to the people of Uganda to warn them beforehand to avoid burying many of them. We also need to care for the suffering with compassion. The orphans and widows need our practical assistance as a demonstration of our Christian commitment. I commend those who are involved in this particular ministry of feeding, clothing, treating and paying school fees of these orphans. Thank you for caring for the widows as well.'

Early in November Edith touched down at Manchester Airport, where Elizabeth Swarbrick picked her up and drove her to Scargill House in Yorkshire. Elizabeth and her friend Pauline Thompson ran a week-long conference on palliative care every year, and St Colomba's Fellowship had invited Edith as their overseas speaker.

The autumn sunshine sparkled as they drove across the Pennines and into the Yorkshire Dales National Park. After a while Edith asked Elizabeth to stop, but not to admire the view. She had spotted something she'd never seen before: dry stone walling. Edith got out of the car for a closer look. 'I'm sure I could use this system on my *shamba*. Who can teach me how to do it?' She was dismayed when Elizabeth told her that even in Yorkshire, where it had been practised for hundreds of years, there was hardly anyone left who knew the art. Edith certainly wouldn't have time to learn it. This was one more idea she would tuck away with all the others that might come in useful one day, a lifelong habit. At Scargill House Edith made good use of the PowerPoint presentation Solomon had helped her to put together. She was such a big hit that the delegates collected a sizeable donation for UWCM. But Edith couldn't stay for the end of the conference. There were lectures she couldn't miss for her degree course, so Elizabeth drove her back to Manchester airport on Thursday night.

Far away in South Wales, the town of Pontypridd had been exploring the possibility of twinning with Mbale. A team visited Mbale to initiate projects such as schools, health care surveys, training of health workers, mosquito nets and goats for vulnerable families, and identified UWCM as a project to be supported. Some with church links paid another visit. They liked UWCM's church-based approach and their practical focus on health. One man wept when he saw Christians who had nothing going out of their way to care for others who had nothing. A Baptist organisation, Seize an Opportunity, teamed up with the Foundation of Development for Needy Communities (started by David's nephew, Samuel) and UWCM to form the Partners Overseas Network Trust (PONT). Finally all branches, civic and church, were brought together as Coalition Against Poverty (CAP).

In Uganda the problem that never went away was staffing. Edith was now in a unique position to speak on the world stage as an authority on the relationship between AIDS, poverty, and a woman's place in society. But to fulfil this role she needed to be free of the daily constraints of Faith House. She had hoped to train Lois as her successor and was horrified when Lois got a job as Child Programmes Officer for CCP.

But there was nothing she could do about it – except shoulder the extra work herself. Sometimes she worked in the office until 8 p.m. Even David felt the strain. Finding a new Executive Director for UWCM became a constant prayer.

When Edith visited YWAM in South Africa again in 2004, her hosts drove her down the spectacular Cape Peninsula road with all its exotic sights: emus, baboons, beaches, penguins, and finally the Cape of Good Hope, where Edith, like all good tourists, had her photograph taken.

UWCM supporters waiting for a newsletter after June 2005 were in for a disappointment. The cost of printing and postage had proved prohibitive. And no-one had time to write and edit one. As AIDS carried on its relentless progress, the number of needy people in the community was increasing.

In March and April 2005, heavy rains washed out many roads, and UWCM's vehicles broke down. Sixty people in the area died of cholera. The office had received 'Macedonian' calls for help from all directions. The strain almost overwhelmed the staff, but by April thirty-two sponsored children were back at school, and the Porridge and Prayer Club had been given ten goats for needy families. There were now ten CMT – three hundred trained CCH.

On her return to Australia, Natasha Edgerton told her boyfriend, Ian Tamplin, all she'd seen and done in Uganda. Her enthusiasm was catching. When his church offered an opportunity to help build houses for an orphanage in Kampala, Ian grabbed it, and when that was finished he spent two weeks with David and Edith. He joined a team of local men to transform UWCM's derelict piggery shed into an office that would be used for LAMPS. On his return to Australia, he asked Natasha to marry him.

Tearfund invited Edith to become a member of their international Partners' Panel for the next three years. This Panel, who help with long-term planning, had members from thirteen different countries. Edith now had the advantage of an annual flight to the UK for three years, and more opportunities to strengthen other overseas links.

One visit gave Edith another opportunity to talk to Bridget Withell.

Bridget's first concern had been the effect of bereavement on women, but she was now worried about the children. Despite the wonderful job Edith and her team were doing, these young people were still suffering. Most were orphans who had been the main carer for a parent dying in appalling conditions. There had been no Children's Conference since 1997 for lack of funds, so Bridget and her church in England raised money to support a four-day residential camp in January 2006.

The towns of Mbale and Pontypridd were officially twinned in May, and on 31 August Edith visited Pontypridd for five days. She received a royal welcome, visited the Welsh Assembly, met many government officials and taught how churches in Uganda work. She set up links between schools, spoke on the local radio and preached at three Sunday services. Edith told the Mayor of Pontypridd and the town council:

'Since the partnership started over 120 goats have been given to the families of orphaned and vulnerable children so that they could help themselves to provide for school fees with the hope of a better future. Over 300 mosquito nets have been provided, the possible consequences of which could be the saving of the lives of over 1000 children through malaria. Eight secondary and four primary schools have already set up partnership links with schools in Mbale, and the churches have forged strong links as well.'

The Council made a handsome donation towards these projects.

Finally a Songs of Praise concert was held in Edith's honour at Rhondda Chapel, Hopkinstown, with the Pontypridd Male Voice Choir. The highlight of the evening was their singing of 'Cwm Rhondda', accompanied by the very organ on which this famous hymn tune was first publicly performed. (PONT newsletter).

CHAPTER 28

2006 ~ a Children's Conference, and more travels

It was a heart-warming sight: more than fifty children aged six to eighteen, all from nightmare home situations, enjoying good food, fun and games for a few days during the school holidays. That's what Bridget Withell and her friends helped to provide when she returned to Uganda in January 2006. At the Children's Conference in a primary school in Mbale the children were taught life skills, but more important, they were helped to express their grief.

One little girl whose father had died in her arms when she was nine, two years earlier, still couldn't look people in the eye. Bridget took her aside for a one-to-one talk. Before the end of the week she was able to cry openly, talk about her loss and grieve for the first time. By charting a family tree the children could see how they fitted in with their extended families, and trace the path of AIDS. They could recognise that as individuals they played an important part. They were taught to care for their own bodies through nutrition, hygiene, avoidance of drugs, sexuality and HIV/AIDS. Each was helped to work out an education and career plan. Practical teaching included sewing, cooking and carpentry.

Bridget trained the adult helpers in bereavement counselling, and they in their turn answered the children's questions. The final joy was a present of blankets and sheets to take home.

Natasha, now Tamplin, returned, bringing her father for a two week flying visit. Mr Edgerton, once in banking, was now a Consultant with World Vision International, and helped her with training and fundraising. Under Edith's guidance the fight against malaria was extended to Bungokho sub-county.

Later in January a group of visitors from the churches of Clevedon spent a few days with Edith. In meeting some of UWCM's clients, they saw real poverty for the first time in their lives. One of the women reported:

'I'd only been in Uganda for three days. I'd expected poverty, but it was still a shock to meet it face to face. Wilson stood tall and proud as he welcomed us to his home. My first thought was that this was the poorest house I'd ever seen. But Wilson was thrilled with it – one of Edith's teams had built it for him. It still needs a door, but it actually had a *corrugated iron roof!* (I learned later that this is luxury; you have to pay craftsmen to fit them.)

'Then on to Florence, a widow, whose home was falling apart, with rain dripping through gaps in the grass roof. With only a thin mattress to sleep on, Florence was dying of AIDS and worried about her six children.

'Margaret and her four children wore only rags handed down from a relative who'd died recently. I fought back the tears as I watched ten-year-old Esther struggling to hold onto her dignity, her only covering a ragged skirt, three sizes too big, slipping off her frail shoulders. When we asked Edith how much it would cost to clothe them, she challenged us, "What good are new clothes when they have no mattress to sleep on and no cooking pot?" Never had I felt so ashamed of my western wealth, so guilty about the possessions I accumulate so casually, or the paltry gifts we'd given them: soap and a flannel for Margaret and soft toys for the children, for which they were so grateful! How could God fail to be angry with the injustice that allowed this little family to live like this, while we and so many others in the world indulge our greed? Shocked into silence, we waited until we were back in Edith's office before we pursued the question. We discovered that for the price of a dinner for two in a restaurant back home (including wine and service) we could provide Margaret with the basics she needed – and some new clothes.

'Finally Edith took us to the Christian Adoption Centre in Mbale, where we met four brothers aged six to fourteen who'd been there for two months. One of the CMT had found them hiding in their home after their mother had died. Their father was illiterate and unemployed. He'd been so ashamed of his inability to provide that he'd simply abandoned them. They couldn't leave the house because they had no clothes. Other kids used to peer through the cracks in the walls and jeer at them. Worse than their loneliness and starvation, they needed hospital treatment for the infestation of jiggers that had eaten away at their fingers and toes. The father had been traced, and he'd agreed for them to be taken to the orphanage. They're still small for their age, but they're learning how to smile and have fun and looking forward to going to school. They'll spend the school holidays with their father, but their welfare will always be monitored by UWCM staff.'

That spring the Gabriel Education Trust contacted Edith. Their mission is to improve the learning environment for children at risk, especially girls, and they needed to identify a project in Uganda with a trustworthy contact on the spot. Bumasamali Primary Boarding School for girls was identified in an almost inaccessible rural area. First they would build a library, then storage. In February 2007 they received a detailed proposal from UWCM. By May, the Trust had already raised £2,250 towards the £7500 they would need by June 2008.

In June Edith was blessed to find two young graduates willing to come on board, despite the low pay and some personal inconvenience. Stephen Gubahama, BA (Public Administration) had a wife and two children in Jinja, but was willing to take a room in Mbale and go home by bus each weekend. Stella Mutonyi Wamai came with a BA (Human Resources Management) and a Dip. Ed (Home Economics and Health, Secondary). Stella had tried to find work in Kampala, but none of the jobs she had been offered (such as in a brewery) had fulfilled her Christian ambitions. To work for Edith she was willing to take a drop in salary. As a thirty-three-year-old woman with two little boys, she knew what women were up against. Stella was a natural for Women's Programmes Officer. She found a carer for her children in Kampala and would visit them twice a month. Just speaking to Edith over the phone to arrange an interview had convinced her that this was the right move.

Stella's chief responsibility was to organise twenty-three groups of women, each about thirty strong, teaching them their legal rights, record keeping, teamwork, nutrition (not *matoke* all the time, please), personal hygiene, reproductive health and family planning. They are also trained as a group to generate income. Sharing their experiences is a great relief to members, who would otherwise have been isolated. New horizons are opening up for them, fresh hope and self-confidence given. Stella visits them every quarter with either Edith or Esther.

Twelve church leaders and members from South Wales came in May 2006 to further the process of church twinning, bringing a BBC Wales TV crew with them.

In a newsletter Edith explained to friends the Day of the African Child, a day dedicated to the memory of the children who died in the Soweto uprising in 1976.

'The 16 June was a prayer day dedicated to the commemoration of the African Child. We at UWCM, during our devotion prayed for all the children in Africa, particularly those orphaned by HIV/AIDS and stricken by poverty. We remembered those dying of malaria in our hospitals and at home. We decided to take action and make a difference for vulnerable children on this day. UWCM distributed some items e.g. milk, eggs and clothes, beddings and dolls to the children's ward in Mbale hospital. Over a hundred little children received these gifts and a smile was realised on the faces of both the children and their caregivers.'

In September Edith was in Oslo for a conference of the Stromme Foundation, a Norwegian government organisation. After the conference, Edith was one of a group taken on the two-hour trip to Geirangah island, a peaceful beauty spot, where they stayed for two days. They were greeted by the Mayor and leaders of the island, which has its own government. After driving back to Oslo through the mountains Edith travelled to Amsterdam, then across the channel to England. In Birmingham for three days she visited Margaret and Frank Wood, who'd been teachers at Nabumali. Margaret introduced her to church friends, and opened a bank account for her so that she could use her Visa card in England.

Next stop was Clevedon, North Somerset, to stay with Terry Game, who had supported UWCM's work ever since she met Edith in Uganda in 1995. This is where I, the writer, come into the story. At Christchurch we heard Edith talk and saw her slides. Afterwards over coffee I spoke to Edith for the first time and told her of my brief visit to Mbale in 1964. Someone asked, 'Isn't anyone writing Edith's biography? They should. It's too good to miss.' Terry Game looked at me. 'You're a writer. Why don't you do it?' Edith pricked her ears up, turned to me with a warm smile, eyes twinkling and asked, 'Yes, why don't you?' We'd only just met and she knew nothing about me. But we both felt that the Lord had his hand on us at this moment. I answered, 'Why not?' Back home I asked my husband what he thought; it would mean a trip to Uganda. Without hesitating Tony replied, 'We'll go to Trailfinders tomorrow and get details.' Within a few days it was all settled. I would fly to Uganda on 4 February 2007.

From Clevedon Edith visited Jane and Laurie Britton and Joan and Fred Parsons in nearby Bristol, all with strong personal and church links with Mbale. Next by bus to Bridget and Stephen Withell in Kent in time for church – and urgent shopping. Edith bought the camera and phone that have been in constant use ever since.

Finally to Tearfund's headquarters in Teddington, where the Partners' Panel met to sort out their priorities. High on the agenda were HIV, children and orphans, and involvement in conflict resolution.

In November Edith was one of the speakers at the fifth International Widows' Conference in Kisumu, Kenya, the theme: 'A widow is a vessel of honour.' Speakers from Uganda Zambia, India, USA and Kenya spoke on:

- Women's and widows' legal rights.
- Prayer life.
- Productivity and financial self-reliance.
- HIV/AIDS and poverty.
- Home based care for the terminally ill.

In February Tamar and Paul presented David and Edith with a healthy, sturdy grandson, Elisha, and later that year David and Edith thanked God when their foster-son Stephen married his good friend, Naomi. They were overjoyed that he'd found someone to love him and provide a stable home life for him. And they loved Naomi, too. Naomi said she had always felt that the Lord had something special for them together.

Samson was getting on well in Cuba, despite moans about the food and the cost of living. Whenever his parents responded to his urgent emails for jeans, warm clothes and toothpaste, the Cuban Embassy helped with delivery. Samson couldn't afford to fly home for holidays, but Canadian friends the McAvitys and Sparlings paid for flights to Canada, where he could both relax and do part-time work.

The eldest Wakumire son, Solomon, had always been a restless soul. After university he went to work in Karamoja and they saw little of him. Christopher, the youngest, was the only one still at home, and still in school. David and Edith sometimes wondered whether their own warm hearts, welcoming so many needy, hurting outsiders into their home, had left their own sons feeling pushed aside. But that hadn't been the case with Tamar. Or perhaps their boys were simply – boys.

By the end of 2006 any other mortal would have needed a long rest, but this is Edith's normal way of life. There was work to be done, and she was the one to do it. Every challenge was an opportunity to develop the work of UWCM, to spread the word and the love of God.

CHAPTER 29

2007 ~ the trek, and my arrival

What, you may have wondered, were seven English men and women doing trekking up Mount Elgon in January 2007? Mount Elgon doesn't present an enormous challenge to anyone with their sights on Everest, but it seemed daunting enough to this inexperienced team. Bridget Withell was the instigator of this four-day trek. Each of them had been sponsored to raise funds for charity, with UWCM as their main objective.

Edith led them to the National Park office in Mbale to 'sign in' and pay the entrance fee. They soon saw why Edith has become such a formidable advocate. The costs were clearly displayed, but Edith protested that these were only for tourists – and four of this party were Ugandans. After much haggling she got a reduction for herself and three young members of her staff. Then Edith refused the tents they were offered. They weren't big enough. They weren't strong enough. Bigger and stronger ones were found. Lastly Edith spotted a large, clear map on the wall. Please could she borrow it? Or could they photocopy it for her? They did.

The team were well prepared and in generally good health. Only when they had reached base camp, tightened their bootlaces, adjusted sunglasses and sunscreen, checked all the equipment and manoeuvred rucksacks onto their backs did they realise that Edith meant to go the whole way with them. They knew she was diabetic and overweight, and when they expressed their doubts, Edith admitted to feeling nervous. David had warned her how steep the cliffs could be above the level familiar to her. However she made a start.

It was an English woman who dropped out first, exhausted and affected by the altitude. Edith volunteered to escort her back to the base, then took her home by bus. But the bus was seriously overcrowded. At the first stop Edith quietly and persistently told the driver that he was breaking the law; he must offload some of his passengers before he went any further. He did as he was told.

Although the expedition had been planned well in advance, communication had obviously been lacking. The team reached first camp after dark to find neither shelter nor food. Terry Game and her husband also suffered from altitude sickness – and blisters – and didn't reach the summit.

A 'Welcome Back and Congratulations' party was waiting for them on their descent. As they stepped into the village hall, each was presented with a flower and a congratulations card. Then they sat down to a feast with fresh pineapples, chicken and fish with groundnut sauce. Edith had even had a T-shirt printed for each of them with the slogan: 'The Great Trek 2007'.

The trek raised over £10,000, which made it all worthwhile. It was agreed that Edith would spend this on seeds and hoes for thirty-five families, school fees for over twenty children, some towards the Children's Conference later that month, the rest to consolidate staff wages.

Bridget Withell reported on the Children's Conference held later that month:

'Our theme: Taking care of yourself. Eighty-one children and young people between the ages of six and nineteen spent a week camping at a primary school in Mbale. They were supported either by UWCM through sponsorship from external donors or through income-generating schemes such as goat rearing. Most had lost one or both parents from AIDS or other causes. Some parents had simply 'disappeared'.

As before, the aims of the conference were to make children feel valued, to provide teaching on life skills, to reduce any sense of isolation or rejection, to 'normalise' their grief experiences, to give an opportunity for peer support and friendships, and to give time for play, free from responsibilities. Also for staff and volunteers to get to know individual children better, and gain a greater understanding of their difficulties.'

Esther Nilly's particular concern was the problems of young girls approaching puberty with no-one to advise them. Traditionally 'aunties' in the villages had taught girls all they need to know about menstruation, the reproductive process and sexuality. But since the onset of HIV/AIDS this tradition has broken down. Today there are many motherless girls and few 'aunties'. It was a relief to be assured that their monthly bleeding was natural and needn't keep them away from school. All they had to do was use a strip of cloth folded inside their knickers that could be washed and re-used. Their frank questioning led to a lot of girlish giggles. One girl asked Esther, 'When I get my pubic hair, can I plait it?' Esther thought carefully for a moment and replied, 'Well you can, but wouldn't it itch? And who's going to see it anyway?' The sound of girlish laughter was a tonic for all.

Last year each child had been given a blanket and sheets. This year it was a paraffin lamp that could be used by the whole family.

No sooner had she waved goodbye to Bridget than Edith was at Entebbe airport to greet me with a warm hug. I was introduced to Andrew, the driver, and soon learned why she valued him so highly. I had lived in Uganda for a year about the time of Independence. I remembered good roads and Kampala as a thriving but relaxed city. We used to drive from Kampala to Entebbe just for fun. But now, after dark, it was no fun at all. The road surface was bad, the traffic chaotic. Obviously a sturdy vehicle and a good driver were essential to Edith's work.

I soon learned the extraordinary way Edith operates. She had booked rooms for us at the Kolping Guest House. It was almost midnight when we checked in. The receptionist gave us our keys, and Edith asked if she could have some tea for her weary guest. The young woman shook her head. 'Sorry, the kitchen is closed.' Edith smiled. 'If you open it for me, I'll make the tea.' The receptionist assured her that it couldn't be done. Edith turned and handed me my key. 'Room 37. You go there and wait for me.' Ten minutes later Edith joined me – followed by a watchman with a tray of tea. On her way to the airport Edith had bought chicken legs, chips and salad. We settled down to enjoy our midnight feast, especially that cup of tea. We were like sisters meeting again after a long separation. This was my first opportunity to witness Edith's formidable combination of thoughtfulness, determination, sweet good-nature – and sense of fun.

In Kampala the following morning we tracked down Jim Sparling at Mengo Hospital. Jim's sixteen-year-old granddaughter, Paula, was staying with him for some weeks, helping to look after the babies. Paula had paid her fare to Uganda by doing holiday work. Jim and Paula were to follow us to Mbale the next day, Jim's twelfth visit to Edith's home.

When Jim showed us around Mengo hospital, desperately in need of funds, I started to understand the grim reality of AIDS. On one of the corridor walls was a large poster showing a picture of a handful of pills, and the message:

> *'From Rhetoric to Reality – Universal Access by 2010.*
> *We have waited too long – We have lost too many.'*

The four-hour drive to Mbale next day confirmed Andrew's worth as a driver. The road offers tantalising glimpses of Lake Victoria, where my husband captained ships in the 1960s, past the Nile Brewery and Owen Falls Dam. There are still square miles of cultivated sugar cane, although most of this once-great industry foundered when Amin expelled the Asians. We passed lorries carrying sugar cane, its stubble still smouldering in the fields. An itinerant trader wobbled along the potholed road, his bicycle overladen with brightly-coloured plastic bowls, baskets and buckets. Large roadside hoardings advertised Sleeping Baby Cosmetics.

The road runs through the fringes of Mabira forest, one of the few remaining pockets of the Guinea Congo Forest that stretched across Africa thousands of years ago, still home to three hundred species and rare primates. And a burial ground for many of Amin's victims. Some scenes of the film *The Last King of Scotland* were shot there. There had been talk of cutting down a quarter of the forest to grow sugar for biofuel production, but protesters argue that this would destroy a unique ecosystem, with consequences for the tourist trade. And others unforeseeable.

On the way through the forest we stopped at a busy roadside

market optimistically known as The Mabira International Hotel, where dozens of traders, all wearing numbered blue tabards, sell just about anything edible – grilled chicken wings, soda pops, pineapples, eggs, live chickens. Once again it was fascinating to watch Edith in action. She was buying for the family, and the price had to be right. She used the same patience and persistence I'd witnessed at the Guest House, examining first one bundle of pineapples, then another, bargaining for the cheapest price. It took a long time, but Edith got what she wanted.

The stretch of road between Jinja and Iganga, narrow and badly-worn, is particularly treacherous. Heavy goods once carried by rail or lake steamer are now carried by road. Aggressive drivers of oil tankers use this route through to Congo and Rwanda, the concentration of traffic ruining whatever road surface remains. There's a popular joke in Uganda:

Q: How do you recognise a drunken driver?
A: He's the one driving in a straight line.

The further we travelled away from the big towns, the more frequently we saw women wearing the *gomas* and carrying burdens on their heads, children walking home wearing school uniform, goats and cows tethered by the roadside.

Edith's home is a three-minute walk away from Faith House, both establishments secure behind high hedges and metal gates. I met the rest of the family – David, Christopher, Esther, Annette and nephew Jonathan. Jim Sparling and Paula joined us the following day.

The ritual for the evening meal is the same every day, no matter how late and how tired people are. In the large living room the food is set out buffet style on a long table, then covered with a cloth. We settled down in comfortable armchairs and settees, all brightened with Edith's embroidered mats. Before tucking in, each of us was invited to thank God for the day's blessings, and raise any personal prayer requests. Esther led us in a song, then 'allocated' prayers, so that everyone's prayer needs were covered. Finally, one of us was asked to thank God for the food, and to bless those who made it. Only then did we go to the buffet and fill our plates. There's always a meat or fish stew with a healthy choice of vegetables, and a variety of local and 'imported' carbohydrates, including chapattis and potatoes, (known in Uganda as 'Irish'.) Finally, those pineapples Edith had bargained for, sometimes mangoes, and always bananas.

I slept comfortably, well fed and under a mosquito net, aware that I'm one of the privileged minority to do so in this country, and only because of Edith and David's great gift for hospitality. It was obvious that visitors are precious to them. Only later did I realise the sacrificial nature of much of the care I received.

CHAPTER 30

2007 ~ a day in the life of UWCM

By the time I finish breakfast Edith has already left for the office, and Andrew has set off for Mbale to collect the staff. This job is becoming increasingly time – and fuel – consuming. He picks them up from a number of gathering points and has difficulty squeezing them all in. At Faith House I find everyone in the main office, ready to start the day with bible study and prayer, using Scripture Union notes. I am introduced to the staff, all eager to tell me about their work.

Stellah, Women's Department, told me, 'If you've done something wrong she never raises her voice or scolds you. With a friendly smile she'll call you for a private talk, then quietly she'll find out what went wrong, and how we can put things right together. You go away feeling "Yes, I can do it." She's made you feel good. There's never any gossiping.'

Mary Wasike, Programmes Manager, had only been there a few days. Thirty-one year old Mary has two children, a fifteen-month old girl at home, and two-months old Elisha, propped up in a cosy chair in the general office, smiling and waving at anyone who walks past him. Mary stops work occasionally to put him to the breast. Other arrangements will have to be made when he's bigger, but being a mother never stopped Edith from working, and Mary was comfortable with the arrangement.

Stephen Gutahama, Human Resources Manager, explained some of their difficulties. There is no budget for administration. Donors like to support one programme per donor, but ignore staff needs. Transport is essential for official trips, especially for Edith. When the truck breaks down, staff have to pay for taxis. All three computers are infected by viruses and too old to update. Since thieves hacked down the power lines there's been no telephone landline, making emailing difficult. Power blackouts happen frequently, especially if someone is welding nearby. They need a three-phase power line. Solar panels are too expensive.

Jaqueline has a diploma in Catering and Hotel Management. Besides general office work she cooks lunch for the staff every day, offering a healthy, varied menu. She is young, pretty and jolly; her smile makes every meal a feast.

Paul and Sam tell me about their work in the Children's Department. Both are graduates, and although for the moment working as volunteers, their approach is entirely professional. Every child is visited and accounted for.

Edith goes to her private office to clear up some administrative business, but her first visitors of the day are waiting outside the door – a widow with a sick baby and six other children. She and two of the children are HIV+. As soon as she has dealt with this family and some paperwork we set off in the pickup. Esther is in charge. She sits beside Andrew, checks her notebook and points the way. This is a normal day's work for her. Edith, Jim, Paula and I are crammed in the back. We skid and lurch along rough, narrow tracks for miles, through small *shambas* of cotton, banana, cassava and other crops, a few houses spaced haphazardly amongst them. Andrew plays a worship tape and he, Esther and Edith join in the singing. After a few miles Esther signals 'slow down', and Andrew parks beneath a mango tree amongst a small cluster of houses. Esther leads us to one.

This is Jacqueline's house. When her husband died of AIDS, his family accused her of infecting him and chased her away. Jacqueline brought her seven children back to her childhood home. At first her uncle squeezed her into his small house along with his own children. But it was a company house, and he had to leave it when his employees sold the business. He could only afford to rent one room. However he'd given his niece a plot of land, and UWCM found the money to build her a house. But they also drew up an agreement, signed by him, promising that she and the children will never be turned out. Her eldest son went back to his father's home, but the other six children are still with her, including three-year-old Isaac.

Today Jacqueline isn't well. She probably has AIDS, and Esther will take her to be tested. UWCM will have to pay £1.50 for this. AIDS patients now fill 70% of hospital beds in Uganda. Isaac sits on her lap, listless, unsmiling. Jim Sparling crouches on a sack outside the house and examines the two. About twenty neighbours gather round. Jim suspects that Jacqueline's head and neck pains are stress-related, and Isaac is clearly undernourished. Jacqueline should be in a clinic, but she has visions of the two of them in a hospital bed, both on a drip. How would she feed Isaac? The other children are at school, so there would be no-one at home to take care of him. An older son, Nakato, is also unwell. Esther makes arrangements to take Jacqueline to the clinic the next day. Jacqueline's widowed mother-in-law joins us. She tells us she does what she can, but has other orphaned children to care for. She's illiterate and doesn't know how old she is. She jokes that when you're pregnant you can count the full moons up to nine, but she's never known a trick for counting the years. Edith thinks she must be eighty-five.

As we return to the truck Jim notices a little boy, aged about three, with a blob of bright pink bowel poking like bubblegum through a hole in his lower left abdomen. A neighbour explains that the boy had an operation for a bowel malfunction. He needs a reversal operation, but is too weak to stand more major surgery. It's hard for a doctor to turn away knowing there is nothing he can do. Jim says that most of the children we see are malnourished. The soil is low in certain minerals such as selenium, and the basic diet of boiled banana or maize meal lacks protein and vitamins. (UNICEF figures for 2005 show that nearly a quarter of under-fives are underweight, and two thirds anaemic. Uganda has the third highest annual population increase after Niger and Yemen. Within the next three years it's expected to have 19.5m children under eighteen.) Esther makes careful notes in her diary.

Back on the bumpy road we go to another village to visit Oliva, a fifteen-year-old schoolgirl. She hasn't come home from school yet, and it's a long walk, so Edith sends Andrew to collect her. Esther talks to the grandmother and looks around the house. Oliva's father has been dead for two years, but her mother died only a fortnight ago. The older brother has gone to stay with relatives, leaving Oliva responsible for four younger brothers and sisters.

Grandmother explains that for the moment she is sleeping in the house with Oliva, Phoebe (fourteen), Samuel (thirteen), Rachel (nine), Richard (eight) and Sharon (six), but she has other orphaned grandchildren and her husband at home, so she can't stay here forever. She points out the graves of family members nearby, including another daughter. Grandfather collects firewood and sells it to buy paraffin, otherwise they would have no light. For 3p you get 100 ml of paraffin (about five tablespoons), enough for one night's light. Oliva does the housework before she goes to school. The house was built by UWCM, but now the grass roof leaks and the door is flimsy. Grandmother showed us the torn mattress cover she had packed with raw cotton to provide a bed for her dying daughter. But now the grey matted cotton spills out onto the floor. This and one torn blanket are the only bedding for the grandmother and six children.

Andrew returns and parks under the mango tree. Out jump Oliva and one of her brothers. They greet the visitors formally, but don't smile. Oliva is clearly distraught, and sits on a mat close to Edith, someone she knows and trusts. Edith puts her arm around the girl. Signs of early womanhood are already appearing. She's an easy prey for any man; all he has to do is break down that flimsy door. The children's school uniforms are filthy. Grandmother explains that these are their only clothes – and she has no soap.

There's also the problem of school fees. Although education is 'free', families are expected to make a 'parental contribution' of £4 per child per annum towards the school's Development Fund. Oliva's grandparents have no way of finding this huge amount. For 17p, when they have it, they can buy a kilo of *posho*, (maize meal), a big part of their diet. To keep a child at primary day school for one year costs about £30. Esther makes a list in her notebook: two blankets (one for boys, one for girls), soap, clothes, pens, books. The house needs a rainproof roof and a lockable door. She'll discuss these, and the cost of schooling, with the team back at the office.

Before we leave Edith says, 'Let's pray', and we do. Between the houses are a number of graves covered with large inscribed slabs. I check the dates on one: Lona was only thirty-four years old. I ask the neighbours for permission to photograph it. They are puzzled at my interest, but don't object. I wonder how much ground that could grow food is filled with graves.

There's one more visit in this village. Forty-five year old Jenny Masete is very sick. Her husband died in 1996. Jenny was given ARV drugs but they made her shake so she had to stop taking them. She can't afford enough food to overcome this common side-effect. Jenny hasn't been able to dig for two years, and often suffers a mental breakdown. UWCM have given her food and encouragement. She has four boys and three girls. UWCM have supported twenty-two-year-old Sam through school. He later trained in brickmaking. He tells us he works whenever he can, earning £1.50 a day, but there isn't much work close to home. If he had a bicycle he could find work in town. But a bicycle costs £30. Esther is twenty. She couldn't finish school for lack of fees. Only two of the girls are at school. There is no money to pay fees for the others. Seventeen-year-old Winnie is mooching around the house. She's supposed to be doing exams, but can't afford the £3 entrance fee for each subject. Jenny's in-laws have lost six children to AIDS, and are left with twenty-one orphaned grandchildren. Once again Esther makes careful notes, and Jim is asked to pray for the family before we leave.

Lastly Andrew drives us to another village, where we stop near a house reaching completion. There we are greeted warmly by a smiling thirty-year-old Jackson and his wife, Lydia. They introduce us to some of their children, including the last born, four-year-old Sam, a sweet, chubby carefree boy with a gorgeous smile. Then we settle down to hear Jackson's story.

CHAPTER 31

Jackson's story, Jacqueline's clinic

Jackson was sixteen when he joined the army. It wasn't a bad life for a teenager. The pay was poor but the uniform was smart, and most nights he had enough in his pocket to fill up with the potent local brew. And all the girls love a man in uniform – especially one with a sergeant's stripes on the sleeve. In the south and west of Uganda, where rebel forces were still resisting the new regime, Jackson made a good soldier. His first marriage was all a bit makeshift. But she was a good girl and he stuck by her, supporting the half a dozen kids she gave him. But of course the army move around, and polygamy was the norm. By the time he was twenty-six, Jackson had married six wives and fathered sixteen children. Then he became sick. Very sick. He deserted. By now he was of no use to the army anyway. Three of his wives and six children died in one year. One wife from another tribe ran away. Only Lydia, the last, stayed with him.

Jackson took Lydia, her thirteen-year-old daughter and four-year-old son, back to his paternal home. His brother took them in. Jackson and Lydia both recovered from TB, but Lydia was HIV+ and Jackson had AIDS. (80% of people with TB are HIV+.) Jackson is a good man, good enough to worry about his motherless children. As soon as he was strong enough he revisited his old army haunts, rounded up eight of his remaining children and brought them back to Lydia. Life wasn't easy with twelve extra people squeezed into his brother's house, but there was nowhere else for them to go. His father was in no state to help: the man who'd once been proud to see his uniformed son go off to war was now so disappointed in him that he'd taken to drink.

At first Jackson was hesitant to ask UWCM for help, and it took some time to persuade him to go to Edith's office and talk to her. It had never been Edith's policy simply to feed the hungry: her aim is to enable the hungry to feed themselves. But this case, like many others, was an emergency. First they had Jackson tested for AIDS and started him on ARV treatment. Then they gave him flour for porridge to overcome the drugs' side effects. But the neighbours got wind of this 'favouritism'. Nobody else was getting a handout. Why should he? They broke into his brother's flimsy house and stole the flour.

Apart from the obvious overcrowding, the brother's house was clearly not secure. UWCM decided he must have his own house, a house built in the traditional manner, but with a corrugated iron roof to keep the rain out, and metal doors and grills to keep the thieves out. They provided the materials, and the family started building the mud walls. The day we called the walls were almost completed, and the floor we sat on was clean and dry. UWCM were ready to provide the roof, doors and windows. After hearing Jackson's story, I was asked to lead prayers before we left.

Julius, the eldest son, has had five years of schooling, but the others very little. During the next few days UWCM enrolled them for school, paid their fees, measured them for uniforms, and gave each one a school bag with exercise books, pens, pencils and a geometry set. I was present when these were given out. Four-year-old Sam was with them, his eyes so wide and hopeful that the staff's hearts melted, and he was given the same. While his brothers and sisters signed a receipt for their bags, I put a pencil between Sam's fingers and guided him to write 'Sam' for the first time, a thrill for both of us.

Jackson's mother helps with the children, and is teaching them how to cultivate the garden. Jackson is still very weak and Lydia does most of the work. They've managed to produce a few vegetables to sell, as well as for their own use, but they weren't well equipped for digging and hoeing. Lydia was looking forward to her new home, but confessed that it was difficult to feed a family of twelve when you had only three plastic plates and mugs. To feed them three at a time takes forever. So UWCM provided bowls, plates and cups, a large bowl for washing and water containers. They were given garden implements and seeds. Jackson's chances of beating AIDS are slim, but he was happy to know that Lydia and the children are safe and provided for.

But there was another problem. Julius is now fourteen, the traditional age for circumcision. For this a goat must be sacrificed – and there was no money for a goat. No goat, no circumcision, and Julius won't be accepted as a man in the community. Edith has strong views on circumcision, but Jackson's family circumstances are very different to her own. She might give advice, but would never force her choice on them.

On the way home from our day of visits, we stop at a rickety roadside shack with the audacious title '*Mombasa Hotel*' painted above the door. Here some entrepreneur fries doughnuts all day long. We buy some for everyone back at the office, a rare treat to enjoy with their afternoon tea. But as soon as tea is over Esther checks her notes: what she saw, what's needed, what it will cost, how they will achieve it. Every item is listed and every penny accounted for. Esther will take care of everything.

Esther goes to Jacqueline's house to take her to the clinic the next day, but the house is empty. Esther assumes she has already left for the clinic. But she needs to make sure, and asks me to go to the clinic with her the following day. She is particularly worried about baby Isaac. Andrew and the pickup aren't available today, so we walk to the main road and wait for a long time for the eight-seater bus. We pay a few pence to be jolted along the road to Mbale, then zigzag on foot through the town's traffic to find St Martin's clinic. We start in the waiting room, then go through every ward. Bizarrely, the music playing somewhere in the background is Abba's *Dancing Queen*. We check every bed, but Jacqueline isn't there. We leave the clinic, retrace our steps across town, find the homeward bus, climb on board – and wait. The driver can't make a profit with only the two of us. Esther buys a paper twist of roasted peanuts and sesame seeds. We wait. One of Esther's cousins climbs on board with a baby boy. The driver is satisfied, and off we go. Esther nurses the baby. We're only five miles from Faith House but Esther's whole morning has been wasted. Or so it seems to me. But Esther is serene as ever. She'll go back to Jacqueline's house tomorrow. In Africa there's always tomorrow.

CHAPTER 32

Canadian friends, the Porridge and Prayer Club

I was curious about an enormous metal container, as big as three houses, parked across the yard from Faith House. One day when we had time to sit down together for a cup of coffee, Edith told me the story.

In June 2006 a lorry carrying the container had miraculously negotiated the tight corner off the Mbale/Tororo road and forced its way along the narrow single track to Faith House, leaving a wake of splintered tree trunks and shredded branches. But that didn't matter: the trees were replaceable, the container wasn't. When the lorry with its precious load trundled through UWCM's wide double gates it was the end of a journey that had started in Canada in August 2005.

The people of Victoria, Vancouver Island, are globally aware and outward looking. And they hate waste. Members of the Victoria Rotary Club were concerned that whenever schools, hospitals or businesses updated their furnishings or equipment, nobody wanted their redundant but still-usable stuff. New equipment was faster, slimmer and lighter, but it seemed sinful to throw the old stuff out for landfill. One member had a few sleepless nights worrying about this. He realised that some developing countries could not afford even the basic equipment, let alone the latest update. From these sleepless nights a workable plan evolved. The Church of Nazarene in Victoria got together with the Rotary Club, hired a huge warehouse and called it the Compassion Resource Warehouse. Medical and school equipment, including books and surplus furniture, are sent there from Vancouver, Calgary and Edmonton, and thirty members of the church congregation work two days a week sorting and packing. They send two full containers a year to developing countries.

It had long been Jim Sparling's dream to send one of these containers to Uganda. Jim had been a frequent visitor to Mengo Hospital since 1966, working there for a few months every year. He knew how sparse and antiquated their equipment was. And in Mbale he had discovered another needy hospital – and UWCM. Jim believes that small group links are more effective than government efforts. And he knew that much of the equipment in the Compassion Resource Warehouse was just what the two hospitals needed. But transport costs money. He put the case to the Victoria Rotary Club, who started fundraising to send a container to Uganda.

Thinking long term, Jim's friends bought a container large enough to be converted into a clinic or store room. A long list was carefully prepared before the mammoth task of documentation and packing began. They found wheelchairs, hospital beds, sheets, school furniture, books and a hundred other things. An extra satisfaction was that David and Edith's son Samson was on holiday with them, and helped with the packing.

The co-operation of the Uganda Customs Office was vital, and Edith began working on this at her end. She had to submit annual budgets and a Memorandum of Understanding to Customs HQ. Back in Canada the contents were packed and listed in such a way that when the container was opened in Kampala, Customs Officers would find everything for Mengo Hospital at the front. These would be removed, the container resealed and sent on to Mbale. Edith made sure that a named senior Customs Officer understood all this, and that he had the necessary file of lists and documents. Nothing was done without his knowledge, and Edith saw with her own eyes that her file was on his desk. Other friends in Canada raised extra money to pay for transport from Kampala to Mbale. The container set out on its journey in November 2005.

By chance, Edith's man was out of town on the day it reached Kampala the following June. The file was on his desk, but none of the other Customs Officers knew about it. So they got to work according to the letter of the law, and unloaded every item. Every single one. From front to back. From top to bottom. Not only the goods for Mengo Hospital, but everything destined for Mbale as well.

This wasn't the only problem. At the time of packing, the friends in Victoria had used their initiative and come up with what seemed like a sensible idea. Instead of buying custom-made polystyrene for packing they used second-hand clothing. It seemed so logical: light, soft and pliant, it made the perfect packing material. And it could ultimately be put to good use in the community. What no-one at either end had realised was that the flourishing trade in second-hand clothing in Uganda is subject to a very lucrative import tax. The Customs Officers were only doing their duty. Every torn shirt, every faded vest, every odd sock was carefully listed, its value on the open market assessed, and charged with import tax. The bill came to the equivalent of about £2,000.

When Edith heard what had happened she was sick with horror. She and David rushed to Kampala, leaving the office to carry on without her. For two weeks they fought their way through a bureaucratic nightmare. Messages flew back and forth between Uganda and Canada. The Victoria Rotary Club paid the huge customs bill. Only then could the container be repacked and sent on to Mbale. (The tax was eventually refunded by the Ministry of Finance in Uganda, but months later.)

And now the container was in place, almost empty. Edith had underestimated the number of helpers and pickup journeys it would take to distribute the contents, and there were still a few odds and ends to unload, but the work was almost done. Jim was gratified when he visited the two hospitals, Mengo and Mbale, and saw wheelchairs, beds and other equipment in place. Once the container was empty it could be fitted with windows and a door and used for storage. The exercise had been worthwhile after all, and some important lessons had been learnt – the hard way.

I was with Jim when he visited Mbale hospital. On the way we had to stop in town to leave a faulty computer at the repair shop, a frequent occurrence. At the hospital Peter, the Paediatrician, showed Jim some push-button aluminium crutches from the container, ready for use when needed. He told Jim, 'That was a commendable job, I tell you. We've had no help from anyone else.' Some of the second-hand clothing had been distributed amongst the sick children. Peter showed us where a new maternity unit, paid for by the Japanese, would soon be finished. This would free up space for paediatric care.

Children would be moved from the acute care ward into the more spacious old maternity unit. We looked in the non-infective children's ward, where every bed was occupied, but Peter told us that this was the 'slack' season. Around April and May, after the rains, four or five children would be packed into every bed. Uganda hadn't escaped the climate changes that are affecting the rest of the world, and the rains have become unpredictable. By now, early February, people should be digging for planting, but the ground was still dry and hard. In nearby Kenya fifty people had already been killed in the first month of the year, fighting over land. Peter and Jim talked about mosquito nets. These are being provided by some organisations, but a new design is needed to protect children in small, crowded homes where all the children sleep on one mat. Jim suggested that local natural plants could be used as anti-mosquito drugs. All this should be decided locally. The USA had donated what seems like a huge amount to fight malaria, but 92% of this was earmarked for research, study and administration – in the USA.

For the past two years on 6 June, the Day of the African Child, UWCM and the Victoria Rotary Club have given 150 litres of milk and thirty trays of eggs to the children of Mbale hospital.

It's no use looking for a 'Casualty' sign here; patients simply sit or lie down on the verandah – and wait. The hospital's white walls are bathed in warm sunshine and shaded with overhanging blossoms of blue Jacaranda, as they were hen Edith was there more than fifty years earlier. It's hard to imagine the distress of families bringing their sick children here. On our way out Peter showed us the dental unit, with its one chair. He told us as we left, 'Among the problems, we work and smile.'

After lunch Edith took Jim, Paula and me to visit the Porridge and Prayer Club (PPC), which has grown and prospered under Sarah Watundu's loving care. It's hard to believe, seeing her energy and beaming smile, that thirteen years ago she almost died of AIDS (Ch 19). Sarah is a sure sign that miracles can and do happen. A hundred and thirteen children, mostly orphans living with grandparents or sick parents, meet for Sunday School and Saturday Club and during the holidays. The children are all tested for HIV, and at the last count only two were positive. Committee members are trained in First Aid, and are sometimes given drug and rehydration kits for common, everyday illnesses. The Club now has a very clear vision: to produce healthy, God-fearing adults with self-esteem. Sarah takes part in a drama programme with TASO which visits schools and churches, using music, dance and poetry to teach about HIV/AIDS. This scheme now includes a pre-school programme for fifty three-to-six-year-olds. Where older children are dropping out of school for lack of fees, they're helped. (Only 66% of boys and 47% of girls complete their primary education at the age of twelve.) The parents, now very much involved, are building a club house. The seed money for this came from donations collected at the funeral of Jim Sparling's mother-in-law, Mrs Price. It's nearing completion, but they're still saving for metal shutters. They hope to employ an instructor to teach handicrafts soon.

And now the grandparents of PPC members have formed a Grandparents Group for mutual support and socialising. They make purses for sale to help support the children. None of this could have been foreseen back in 1994.

A formal welcome has been arranged for us in the village hall, where we VIPs are seated on a dais. A visit from 'Mama' Edith is obviously a great honour. She introduces Paul, new to UWCM's Children's Department, with special responsibility for secondary students. She tells them, 'Esther will still visit and pray for you, but take your school reports to Uncle Paul. He will visit schools and homes. If you work hard at school, it makes it easier for God to do what he plans for you. And it will make a big difference in the village in the coming years.'

Edith tells the children that they're the most important people here, but today Jim is the Guest of Honour, and Edith introduces him and Paula. Some of the children have forged personal links, and Jim has bought letters and small gifts from their friends in Canada. He has brought every child a bright red T-shirt, specially inscribed to wear at the club. Some of the older children tiptoe out, and there are a few minutes of waiting and whispering before they march in, with drums, wearing their new T-shirts, singing, 'I love you Jesus, you are my Saviour', and then:

> 'We are happy, dear visitors, it's really a wonderful day.
> We are happy to receive you, we wish you long life,

Dear visitors, we promise to pray for each other'.

Their voices are sweet, and their whole bodies move as they sing and chant. Seven seniors step forward to sing 'When the Saints Come Marching In', and lastly all join in:

'Lord Jesus I love you, you know I love you,
Lord Jesus, you saved me from sin and shame.
You give me power at every hour.
Lord Jesus, I love you, you know I do.'

There are speeches of welcome, and pride in the PPC shines from every face. After these ceremonies there's time to relax, and Edith, Paula and I are asked to help distribute the day's porridge. We scoop it from huge drums out into large, brightly coloured plastic mugs. It's heartwarming to see all those wide smiles, moustached with porridge. There's a little left, and we try some: it tastes good. This was probably one of the days when a little extra is added – milk, honey or sugar. There was a rumble of thunder while we were in the hall, but the threatened rain doesn't materialise. A little would have been welcome.

The following day Jim and Paula leave for Kampala by bus. We hear later that it breaks down half way, and they have a two-hour wait for a replacement. The four-hour journey has taken over six hours. For me, there's a different journey of discovery.

CHAPTER 33

Nancy and the school

Today I have Andrew and the pickup to myself. He drives me south to Bumasikye Child Development Centre, Nancy's place of work, and leaves me there for the day.

When Nancy's mother died Nancy was five, and her sister, Annette, six months old. The Wakumires made Annette their legal foster-daughter. Their father could cope with the other six children – just. He never married again, knowing how easily a stepmother can break up a family.

Although not strictly a foster-daughter, Nancy has always regarded Edith and David as Mum and Dad, as well as friends. When her school results were poor, Edith encouraged her. When she was growing up and needed pocket money, Edith taught her to embroider tablecloths for sale. Nancy told me, 'I really thank God for Edith's big, warm heart, a place of refuge for a motherless girl. All the self-esteem I have I learned from her. She used to give me small gifts – a pair of knickers, some face cream and a handbag, a modest bank note hidden in a Christmas card. I used to be so shy. Then one day at a Children's Conference she asked me to stand up and tell the other girls about personal hygiene. And I did! Until then I could never have imagined myself speaking in public. She really boosted my self-confidence.'

David and Edith watched over Nancy and helped her financially until October 2006, when she graduated with a BA in Social Administration. She started work immediately as Project Director of Bumasikye Centre. Nancy still calls in at the Wakumire home several times a week.

The Centre was set up two years ago in this rural setting by Compassion International, whose headquarters are in Kampala. Alongside the office building is a well-equipped children's playground. Trees have been planted that will soon give a little shade. Children aged three to eleven meet for fun and games every Saturday, and three days a week during school holidays. They are taught PE, spirituality, handicrafts and emotional skills with the help of games and puzzles.

But this is more than a playgroup. A committee of local people plan and budget for the year. They work well together, visiting homes to identify the needs of individual children. Files in the office hold details of every child, including a map showing where each one lives. Children between the ages of three and seven are visited three times a year, the others once a year until they're twenty-two. Committee members talk problems over with care-givers. They have links with TASO, and test both children and carers for HIV/AIDS. The Centre's staff includes a Health Officer, a Finance Director and a Sponsored Donor Officer. Nancy, their Accountant as well as Project Director, has her own private office. The aim of the Centre is clearly displayed on the office wall:

'To release children from holistic poverty by equipping them and unwrapping their God-given talents and gifts into fulfilled Christian adults who can change their community for the better.'

The children are encouraged to be ambitious and aim for university. The President of Compassion International says, 'Whenever a child comes to you it's a divine appointment.'

A few yards from the Centre is Bumasikye Primary School, where I met Sarah, the Headmistress. As I approached the school I was astonished to see a large notice board with the words:

'VIRGINITY IS GOOD FOR BOYS AS WELL AS GIRLS'

Nobody could miss it – which was the whole point.

From the outside there isn't much to distinguish one school in Uganda from another. White painted single storey huts, some freshly painted, some neglected, stand out from the surrounding green fields.

As you pass some schools, children can be heard chanting 'Two times two is four, three times two is six', and counting to the beat of a drum. But this school is much more advanced.

Some schools have up to 2,000 pupils: Bumasikye School has 800. Universal free primary education has been the norm since 1997, so although Bumasikye was founded by the church, staff salaries are paid by the government. But there's a snag. Staff salaries are only one item in a school's expenses. Parents are asked to pay formidable extras. First there's the Parents' Contribution, a fee in all but name, which covers maintenance and all other costs. Then there's the uniform and materials such as exercise books, pens and pencils. And when a child reaches the end of school and wants something to show for it, the examination fees can be crippling.

Here every facility is used to the maximum. The white external walls have educational pictures painted on them. On one is a well-drawn picture of the human body, larger than life, with all its parts clearly named. And that slogan that caught my eye (above) is on a board hammered into a grass verge that every child must pass every day.

The school is well maintained, with lemon and mango trees providing shade. I visited a class of more than fifty, the official upper limit. They have a staff of only fifteen, and can't find the extra two they need. Few qualified teachers live within easy reach of any rural school. Transport, whether public or private, is either difficult or unobtainable. At some schools teachers don't turn up until mid day, as tired and hungry as the children. Some children at Bumasikye walk four kilometres to school, and the teachers even further. Many of the children are too poor to bring food, so the school has to feed them.

Bumasikye is open to all. The Muslims who send their children are aware that this is a Christian school, but are happy for their children to be taught Christian values. There is neither segregation nor compulsion. Muslims, Catholics and Orthodox go to church with the rest every Wednesday. Membership of the SU Club is optional.

When Sarah came as headmistress in April 2005, she was puzzled and disturbed by the bad atmosphere at the school. Teachers had been turning up late. There had been a lot of truancy, especially on market days, when children would help their parents at the market. Some of the children's behaviour had been particularly strange. Sarah did some sleuthing, and discovered that a trading centre in a nearby town had been exposing the children to late night pornographic video shows. They had seen things on screen that they would never have otherwise imagined. For some of them this was a novelty that had to be explored. Sarah had to work very hard to turn things around in two years.

Sarah wants to build staff houses, but the community also needs a new church and a house for the pastor. She told me, 'Often I have to turn beggar, or pay for items out of my own salary.' Her next ambition is to buy crystal radio for the school. Many parents are suspicious, seeing the government and NGOs such as Save the Children as a threat to their authority.

During my last two days at Edith's home, we spent as much time as we could together. Even after all I'd seen for myself, many of the facts I jotted down during these sessions came as a shock. Edith's energy is awe-inspiring, but there were times when she would say, 'Just give me fifteen minutes', and close her eyes – for ten.

She told me that domestic violence 'within reason' is tolerated, and the Domestic Relations Bill drafted in 2000 was still not passed. Multiple marriages and the marriage of young girls aren't illegal and schooling isn't compulsory. Amongst females aged fifteen to twenty-four, 4.3% will develop HIV/AIDS against 1% of males. But Edith believes husbands are becoming more supportive and traditions slowly changing. Christian women are refusing to be 'inherited', men are recognising their wives' ability to share responsibility, and are writing wills ensuring their security.

I met Edith's eldest sister, Florence, now a gracious elderly widow who speaks little English. But Christine, now retired, still leads an active, forceful life. She told me; 'Single women, widows and youths are still not given full respect, even in the church. Although I was Secretary to the Mayor of Mbale for years, if I stood for election now people would say; "But she's not married; what is she going to do for us?" A single woman will often attach herself to any man rather than be left single.'

We visited Bishop Samwiri Wabulakho, who chuckled when he told me about his work as one of the first CCH, marching out to spread the gospel armed with disinfectant and rubber gloves. He told me, 'Edith's work definitely started with the church. I've seen God at work; many have been converted through her evangelistic outreach. Orphans and women who'd lost hope have recovered it. The CMT are going to the grass roots to combat poverty, ignorance and disease.'

At Nabumali I met Grace and John Molli (Ch 8). We strolled past a group of men, drinking, smoking and talking just as Bridget had described them. John grinned, 'They'll be discussing our *mzungu* visitor and wondering what you've brought us.' I told him, 'Tell them this *mzungu*'s lost her air ticket, and was asking you for a loan to get home.' It was lovely to see Edith relaxing and joking with these old friends. As one of her friends has said, if you could bottle her laughter, you'd make a million.

Finally a visit to Beatrice, Edith's dressmaker, who fitted me with a beautiful long, lined skirt in a cotton African print.

For my last three days we stayed at the Catholic Church guest house in Kampala. There were power cuts (hurricane lamps in every room) and water cuts (buckets of water in every bathroom), and the traffic scared me rigid. It seemed impossible to get across Kampala without seeing someone killed. But we did, and had a great time. We had lunch with Tamar and her two lovely children, met her husband Paul outside the once-notorious AEE offices, the building used by Idi Amin's SRB. We had tea with foster-son Paul at the Sheraton. We met Stephen and Naomi Watiti, a couple obviously in love. Sarah Inero (Ch 14) gave me one of her delightful music tapes. I saw Edith reunited with Esaza (Ch 15) on her son's first birthday. It was wonderful to see the love between 'Mama Edith' and all her beloved children. There was much laughter – and food – when we visited her sister Margaret and husband John. Archbishop Henry Orombi was gracious enough to break off a meeting to talk to us, and on Sunday morning we heard him speak (and sing) at morning service at All Saints' Cathedral.

Edith had the room next to mine at the guest house. On the second day I could hear her on the phone, speaking loudly, then sing the hymn '*Amazing Grace*'. Very strange. A moment later she knocked at my door. 'That was my sister Freda from Massachusetts. She's with an old friend who's very ill, and wants to hear '*Amazing Grace*' once more before she dies. She's not sure of the words and I don't know whether I've got them all. Do you know them?' I thought I could remember most of them. We sat down on my bed and sang the hymn through while she made notes. Then she went back to her room, rang her sister, and sang 'Amazing Grace' slowly, all the way through.

It was my last day and I was flying home that evening. All I had to do was finish my packing, have a light snack, and set off for Entebbe airport. We were on our way back to the guest house when Edith shouted, 'Stop.' Andrew pulled up outside a petrol station. As Edith got out I started to follow, but she asked me to wait, disappearing inside a small corner shop next to the petrol station. Andrew and I waited. We looked at our watches. The sun was sinking. We looked at our watches again. I got out of the pickup and went into the little shop. Edith wasn't there. But from the rear of the petrol station I could hear her voice. She was deep in conversation with the builders of a large shed nearing completion, scribbling in her notebook. I called out, pointing to my watch. At that moment I might have been on another planet. Registering my presence at last, she pointed to the roof of the shed, thatched with a tight, clean thatching very different to the drooping roofs I'd seen in the villages. 'I'm just getting all the details; I won't be a moment.' At last she thanked the men profusely, then joined me and walked back to the car. 'That's just what I need,' she said triumphantly. She didn't elaborate, but later I could see why she was so interested.

I later discovered that she'd gone into that shop to buy two cards – a farewell card for me, and one for Tony, thanking him for letting me come.

I'd only been back in England a few days when Freda phoned from Massachusetts. She'd just been to the old lady's funeral. Her friend had died in peace, the words of 'Amazing Grace' some of the last she'd heard before joining her Maker. Then Freda told me some hair-raising stories about her time with Idi Amin.

Since my visit Jacqueline and her sons Nakato and little Isaac (Ch 29) have died, so has Jackson's wife, Lydia (Ch 31). Jackson is still alive and working to feed the children, but he now regards UWCM as his family and they help him with extra food. Sarah Watundu (Ch 32) is still well and smiling at Sakyia.

CHAPTER 34

The future

After Natasha and Ian Tamplin returned to Uganda in May 2007, thieves broke into their Mbale home and stole the laptop that had all their planning and assessment work on it. Even more distressing, one of their young guard dogs was killed. This was a major setback, but the work goes on. Although sponsored by TEAR Australia, Natasha is now proud to be an official member of the UWCM staff.

In September 2007 Edith was back in the UK. When she spoke at Tearfund's HQ she was able to report:

- There are now fifteen trained teams of thirty volunteers, each caring for five families. With an average of five members per family, that makes a total of 15 x 30 x 5 x 5 = **11,250 individuals** being cared for on a regular basis. At least sixty-five of those volunteers are now men.
- Sixty church leaders have been trained on integral mission.
- Sixty teenage mothers have been given knowledge, skills and resources to enable them to handle life's challenges more positively. Each has been given a goat to improve the nutrition of their child and raise some income.
- 135 children are being supported in thirty-six homes. Some have parents living with HIV/AIDS, three homes have ten children each, some are child-headed homes with no relative showing sympathy.
- About fifty women are now in local government leadership positions.

- 295 women who are HIV+ now speak publicly about their experiences. Sixteen of them are considering going back to school, and one, a widow with eleven children, was about to sit the national O level exams.
- 3,174 orphans and vulnerable children have been supported with both formal and vocational education skills. Twenty have been given goats. The number of dropouts in supported schools has reduced.
- In three communities, UWCM in partnership with Stromme Foundation have provided schools with two staff quarters, three pit latrines, two kitchens and a furnished classroom.
- Three hundred children under five have been given mosquito nets. Health workers have promoted primary health care and prevention measures among orphans and vulnerable children and the community at large.
- Thirty-two children are receiving help with school fees and scholastic materials through personal sponsorship.

Edith went on; 'After witnessing UWCM's church-based intervention, whole families are turning to Christ. The church is now seen as a place of hope. CMT can mobilise resources and support from the congregation to reach out to those in need, especially vulnerable children and women and people living with HIV/AIDS. Loss and death are real, but the church has hope. It is a powerful force in fighting against HIV/AIDS.' She had more personal stories to tell:

Oliva (Ch 30), now newly-clothed and in a house made secure, had told her: 'I thought that I would never go to school this term, but God is great!'

Home renovation has kept vulnerable families dry and secure. Robert's four-year-old son looked around after UWCM had improved their home and asked, 'Is this our house?' All this expenditure comes out of general funds.

Pius, one of their sponsored teenagers, was killed with three others on a building site when the pit they were digging collapsed. He was just about to begin an industrial training course to support his two sisters.

Fifteen-year-old Caroline lived in the slums of Mbale. When her parents developed AIDS, Caroline was pulled out of school to care for them. Her little brother was still at school. Desperate to keep a roof over their heads, Caroline started brewing *busera*, a dangerous trade for a teenage girl. UWCM encouraged her to buy and sell produce instead, but she was drawn into prostitution and became pregnant at seventeen. Edith urges that someone must care and speak for these thousands of children, teach them self-worth and give them empowerment.

Geoffrey was desperately ill and Grace, his first wife, was pregnant. His second wife had died leaving a two-month old baby, Peace. There were ten other children. UWCM had them all tested for HIV+ and provided food and counselling. Geoffrey and Peace are on ART and Grace on Prophaxis. The older children now earn money by crushing stone and collecting firewood.

Mooli Chris became a Muslim during the Amin regime. His wife died, leaving four children. UWCM referred him to TASO and he's now on ART. He has recovered his Christian faith, and has high hopes for the two daughters still living with him.

Edith's three weeks of travel included a Tearfund regional conference at Taunton, Somerset. Back in Clevedon Edith spoke in two churches and David preached at Christchurch. His text was the parable of the wheat and weeds from Matthew 13. The congregation also joined in a hymn written by David, 'Love is the greatest thing'.

That Sunday morning Edith wore a colourful gown similar to the one she had worn for her presentation at the United Nations. But between the hem of that gown and her sensible black shoes I caught a glimpse of Walt Disney socks with a picture of Tigger and the legend, '*Look before you bounce*', which seemed very appropriate. In my home she examined our simple but effective shower system. How much did the showers cost? How easy were they to install? Where could she buy them? Even now she was thinking about those guest houses waiting to be completed back in Uganda. After spending a few valuable hours with me checking details of her story, Edith left with David for Bristol, Grimsby, Cheshire, Preston and Powys. The couple flew back to Uganda on 14 October.

The Devil doesn't like it when Christian plans are going well. Three days before they left England David's brother, Pastor Christian Emmanuel

Peter, phoned from hospital in Uganda to say goodbye. He had had a heart attack, and knew he wouldn't see David again. All David could do was to help make arrangements for the funeral by telephone.

They arrived home to be faced with a more immediate problem. The day before their return, thieves had cut down their electricity cables. The soaring price of second-hand copper is creating havoc all over the world, but here even the poles had been stolen. One huge relief was that because the theft had happened outside their compound, they would not have to bear the cost of replacement. However they endured a week of chaos, with no power either in the office or at home, and all computer systems out of action. But worse was to come.

On Friday 26 October David was in Kampala when Edith received a phone call from the police. A head-on collision of taxis on the notorious stretch of road between Iganga and Jinja had caused ten fatalities, one of them Stephen Gubahama, her Assistant Finance Officer. Would she please come and collect the body?

Edith's first instinct was to phone David. He arranged to meet her at the police station, but told her to drive to Mbale first and buy a coffin. Andrew drove her and the coffin to meet David at the police station. Together they put Stephen's body in the coffin and took him home to his wife, Elizabeth. Many UWCM staff were at the funeral on Sunday, but Edith closed the office on Monday. They all needed time to grieve and pray. And there were practical arrangements to be made for the care of the family. Stephen's twelve-year-old son Joel was to take his Primary Leaving exams the following week. Then there was Rita, aged ten, and four other dependants to be taken care of.

Since April 2007 there has been heavy flooding in some regions. Bridges have been washed away, and many towns such as Soroti have been cut off. Displaced people within UWCM's area have had to erect rough temporary shelters. Left without food, they struggled to reach what was left of their crops by canoe. Epidemics of cholera and dysentery have broken out in various places.

Landslides around Mount Elgon killed a hundred and left five hundred homeless. Trees, crops and topsoil were washed away. Many coffee plants were destroyed, stripping people of their only cash resource. Troubles in neighbouring Kenya brought thousands of refugees across the border, raising the cost of petrol and making food even scarcer.

The Mbale region has been touched by the Ebola infection that broke out in various parts of the country. President Museveni has told people that in future he'll have to simply wave to them instead of shaking hands. But there's much cause for hope.

The long struggle to prevent the loss of part of the ancient Mabira forest for sugar has been won – for the time being.[1]

Entebbe airport and roads around Kampala were renovated and cleared for the Queen's visit in November. Stephen Watiti, now Senior Medical Officer at the Mildmay Centre in Kampala, was proud to show the Queen around when she visited the clinic. When Stephen isn't working he speaks, especially in churches, mostly to combat HIV-related stigma.

In Uganda it's impossible to read after the sun goes down at about 7 p.m. without costly light. Power failures plague the computer systems in UWCM's offices. But the Lighting Africa initiative has been drumming up competition for providing low cost green lighting products for low-income consumers in sub-Saharan Africa. This could have an impact on UWCM's communities out of all proportion to the cost.[2]

Uganda was one of the first countries to respond positively to the HIV/AIDS crisis and pioneered the 'ABC' approach: Abstinence, Be faithful, wear a Condom. But Beatrice Were of ActionAid reports, 'Now, under the influence of US donors, often driven by the evangelical right, billboards have been replaced by marches of virgins, and proposals for university scholarships for those who remain 'untainted'. There is a new wave of stigma in the country.'[3] President Museveni has called for the spread of HIV/AIDS to be a punishable offence. And yet where one partner in a monogamous relation is HIV+, only a condom can protect the other partner. (Since April 2007 adultery is no longer illegal for women – another step towards equality.)

Edith has a new vision for the future, a community sponsorship scheme to help families to become independent as well as giving practical help. When income-generating activities begin to pay off, women can approach them for interest-free loans with long repayment periods, still making a profit while repaying the loan. Lastly, low-interest loans to relatively well-off women running small businesses, plus training in financial and small business management.

She says, 'Individual child sponsorship has always been popular. Supporters love to have a photograph of 'their' little boy or girl, and to know what progress they are making at school. But it brings a problem – jealousy. There's limited value in sending one child to school if others have to stay at home, lacking essentials. And this can affect the whole community. I would like more donor help to go directly to the grassroots women, not through bureaucracy. Women should have a choice in what they do. When they own and participate in a project it is more likely to be sustained.

'There are still some questions to be answered. Will sponsors be satisfied if their contribution is shared amongst several families rather than one family or individual? Will they be happy to know they've provided perhaps a new roof for one and farming tools for another? The success of this project depends very much on finding the right paid staff and volunteers.

'But for all this, UWCM needs more money from outside sources. We've been forced to give two cows instead of fifteen to a group of thirty women. We're only scratching the tip of the iceberg.'

The six self-contained guest houses near Faith House have been completed. They will be let out to visitors, providing UWCM with a small income. From the outside they are typical rondavels, but with comfortable beds, mosquito nets, tiled floors, toilets – and no doubt thatched roofing like that she spotted in Kampala, and showers like mine in England.

The future of the Ebenezer Centre is still uncertain, but a Cayaple hedge has been planted round it. Volunteers have built a conference hall on what used to be the piggery compound.

On 6 July 2007 Edith was awarded a degree at Mukono Christian University. Demands on her time are still relentless. In 2008 Oxfam invited her to speak at three events in South Wales on climate change and its impact on agriculture in Africa. She and the First Minister, Rhodri Morgan, presented the Gold Star Community Awards at the Cardiff Eisteddfod, celebrating 'the extraordinary contribution of ordinary people and communities in Wales to global poverty and justice.'[4] In September she and Nancy began a course for a Master's degree in Organisational Leadership and Financial Management.

Edith is now open to whatever uses the Lord has for her skills and experiences. She sees UWCM as a viable body in its own right, with a staff of seventeen no longer needing her day-to-day administrative skills. Lois (chapter 27) is back with UWCM, and at last being trained to take over from Edith as Chief Executive. As well as her global work, Edith is looking forward to spending more time as a wife to David, a mother to her four children and seven foster-children, and grandmother to a growing number of grandchildren.

Much of my research has been done by phone and email since my visit, but I trust I have given a sufficiently truthful picture of Edith's remarkable story to whet your appetite to learn more about the important issues raised, and the work of UWCM.

Those small feet that once climbed the bamboo forests of Mount Elgon have grown, but there are now even higher mountains to climb. There are still challenges that might have crushed a weaker heart and quenched a less generous, loving spirit. All her life Edith has given that heart and love to every man, child and woman who is physically, emotionally and spiritually abused, but her first commitment is to her loving Heavenly Father and His Son, her Saviour, Jesus Christ.

[1] *Independent, 10/07/07*
[2] *Independent, 28/8/7*
[3] www.actionaid.org.uk
[4] *Western Mail, 02.08.0*

BIBLIOGRAPHY

Allen, John, *Rabble Rouser for Peace* – Random House, 2006, ISBN 1844 135713

Coomes, Anne, *African Harvest – the story of African Enterprise*, Monarch, 2002, 1SBN 1 85424 599 6

Kivengere, Bishop Festo, *I love Idi Amin* – New Life Ventures (Marshall, Morgan & Scott), 1997, ISBN 0 551 05577 4.

Kyemba, Henry, *A State of Blood* – Fountain Publishers Ltd, Kampala, 1997, ISBN 9970 02 132 X

Pollock, John, *The Billy Graham Story* – Zondervan, 2003, ISBN 0 310 25126 5

Waite, Terry, *Taken on Trust* – Hodder & Stoughton, 1993, ISBN 0 340 60969 9

About the Author

Margaret Spivey was born in Yorkshire, married the boy next door, and lived in London before moving to East Africa, where her husband, a Marine Officer, worked on the lakes for fourteen years. She had been a Secretary, but on her return to England took evening classes to make up for a failed school certificate, qualified for college as a mature student, and trained as a teacher. She and their young son and daughter then went with her husband to Fiji for eight years. There she spent three years teaching at the grammar school and played an increasingly active role in the theatre.

Since her teens Margaret has been involved in drama, whether as back row of a Gilbert & Sullivan chorus, playing a serious role, being the pantomime fairy or directing Murder in the Cathedral – in a cathedral. She was a story-reader and presenter in Radio Fiji's schools broadcasts unit.

Back in England Margaret joined the Association of Christian Writers, started writing books for children, and was a regular contributor to Scripture Union's children's work for twelve years. One of her books is a teaching aid for Old Testament studies. She has produced a steady output of short stories, sketches and magazine articles, and won two poetry prizes.

Margaret is an active Christian and church member, and has taken part in missions in Northern Ireland and other places. She believes passionately in the work Edith Wakumire is doing. Her Christian beliefs and love of Africa have led her to write Edith's biography, and she is confident that the time it has taken has been time well spent.

When Margaret is not writing she shares retirement with her husband, which includes enjoying one grandson in England and visiting two in Australia.

Lightning Source UK Ltd.
Milton Keynes UK

175564UK00002B/34/P